how to be a great Mum

tracey godridge

foulsham

LONDON • NEW YORK • TORONTO • SYDNEY

foulsham

The Publishing House, Bennetts Close, Cippenham, Slough,
Berkshire, SL1 5AP, England

Foulsham books can be found in all good bookshops and direct from
www.foulsham.com

ISBN: 978-0-572-03213-5

Copyright © 2007 Tracey Godridge

Cover photograph © Superstock

A CIP record for this book is available from the British Library

Printed in Great Britain by Creative Print and Design (Wales), Ebbw Vale

Contents

For Martin, Cora, Eden and Noah

Introduction

You are going to be a mum. Whether you have planned this for ages or it comes as a thrilling surprise, the chances are you'll be overwhelmed by a flood of feelings: wonder, joy, excitement, confusion. Your life suddenly feels richer and broader than you ever imagined. Yet at the same time you are anxious and protective. Can you ever measure up to the needs of your child? Can you ever be a great mum?

No one would argue that being a parent isn't a huge responsibility. In fact, given all the big issues parents are regularly confronted with in the media (obesity, teen pregnancies, drugs, bullying) it's amazing anyone still chooses to have children. So how can you avoid being overwhelmed by all the inevitable worry? I remember my own mother saying once, when I was fretting about which school to send my daughter to, 'When you were little, all we worried about was keeping you warm, well fed and well loved'. And she was so right. Focus on these absolute essentials – keeping your child healthy and happy – and you can feel confident that you really are doing a great job.

Of course, what your child needs to stay healthy and happy will change as she grows and develops – and recognising your child's changing needs will be the best way of helping her stay this way. How, for example, can you encourage your stubborn toddler to love good food? Who's the best person to care for her if you go back to work? How can you get your sluggish nine year old to exercise more? What's the best way to boost your teenager's sense of self?

Hopefully the information, advice, tactics and strategies offered here will help get your child off to a great start in life –

encouraging habits that will keep her fit and healthy throughout her life, and equipping her with the confidence and self-esteem she needs to become a happy, capable and independent young adult. And while being a mum – especially a great mum – from the moment of conception right through to adulthood, will inevitably be challenging, hopefully it will also be as exciting, fun and rewarding as you ever imagined it would.

When you are talking about children, it's really annoying to keep writing 'he or she' and 'him or her' – and annoying to read, too. For this reason I have switched between the two from chapter to chapter. I hope we are way beyond believing that boys can't cook and girls don't know the offside rule, so whether you have sons, daughters or both, I'm sure you can substitute 'he' or 'she' as necessary.

Tracey Godridge is a journalist and author specialising in birth and parenting. She has worked for many years as an editor and consultant editor on top-selling national parenting magazines, and continues to contribute regularly to parenting magazines and websites. She is also the author of a number of childcare books. She has three children, currently aged nine, twelve and fourteen. If you would like to send her your thoughts and ideas on *How to be a great mum* she'd love to hear from you. You can visit her website at www.traceygodridge.co.uk.

CHAPTER 1

What Is a Great Mum?

The most important answer to this question is that a great mum isn't the same as a perfect mum. Children don't need perfection, and even if they did, no mum could be perfect. Even trying would make you feel miserable because it would mean never making a mistake, and that is neither possible nor desirable!

Being a mum involves such a huge range of roles – cook, nurse, teacher, counsellor, mediator, taxi driver, careers advisor – that getting it wrong sometimes, and not always having the answers, is inevitable. Also, you are learning on the job. There's no formal training and no dry run. One day you're pregnant, the next you are cuddling your newborn and trying to get to grips with breastfeeding.

But while no mum should try to be perfect, every mum can be great. How? Of course, there are numerous ways: having a great sense of humour and endless patience; being warm and kind, positive and fun. But if you had to pick out the most important traits, which are the ones that would really make a difference to your child? Here are a few suggestions.

1 Loving your child without strings attached

Being loved builds confidence, but only if the love is unconditional. This means making sure your child knows that you love him whatever – whether he breaks your favourite vase, flunks his exams, dyes his hair red or refuses to eat his peas. He needs to be certain that your love doesn't depend on the way he looks or behaves, and that it won't be used as a threat or a reward. This doesn't mean that you can never get angry or frustrated, just that your child should know that it is his behaviour, not him, that you don't like.

2 Talking to your child openly and honestly

Love and trust go hand in hand. The more honest and open you are with your child, the more he'll trust you, and the more loved and secure he'll feel. Developing a strong, close bond with your child in this way will also help form a pattern for his relationships throughout life. This means being understanding and patient, especially when helping to sort out his worries and confusions. It also means listening without judging. He needs to feel safe about asking questions and speaking his mind, even when his point of view is different to yours.

3 Valuing the time you spend together

As a mum, especially when your child is young, you'll often feel as if you have little time to yourself. But it's how you spend time with your child that counts. Ignoring the chores for half an hour and sitting down to listen to your son tell you about his latest craze will be worth more to him than a whole day being in the same house together but in different rooms. Time spent interacting with your child shows that you value his company, which in turn will boost his self-esteem and help him feel valued and worthwhile.

4 Keeping your child fit and well

Making sure you child is safe, warm, fed and clothed is an everyday priority. But thinking ahead about your child's health is important too: the habits formed now will have a big impact on the quality of his adult life. Research shows, for example, that active children are more likely to remain active in later life. Similarly, encouraging your child to eat his greens today means he's more likely to eat a healthy diet as an adult.

5 Nurturing your child's skills and abilities

To help him get the best out of life, your child needs to discover his potential. This doesn't mean pushing him to run before he's ready to walk. Instead it means finding ways to stimulate and support his interests and abilities – with books, activities, new experiences, plus plenty of encouragement and praise. Focusing on what he can realistically achieve will help him feel good about himself and motivated to take on greater challenges.

6 Setting a good example

As scary as it sounds, when it comes to teaching your child about how to behave in the world, you are his first and most important role model. From his earliest moments he'll be watching you – how you speak, how you behave and the things you do will shape his development for the rest of his life. So if, for example, you want your child to value other people, to enjoy reading and to respect the environment, then he needs to see you being affectionate with your partner, choosing a book instead of the television and walking to the shops instead of jumping into the car.

> *'Before Phoebe was born I was much more selfish and impatient. Becoming a mum and wanting to do a great job has really changed me for the better.'*
>
> Sian, mum to Phoebe, aged four

Learning as you go

Becoming a great mum takes time and experience, and there are bound to be occasions when circumstances (stress at work or a string of broken nights) undermine your efforts. When this happens, good support strategies can do wonders for your ability to cope.

● Talk to people you trust: your partner, family, friends. Sharing difficulties with other people can help you to see them in a new and often less negative light.

- Make friends with parents who have children the same age. Knowing that you are not the only one facing a particular problem or challenge can make the world of difference, and they may have ideas that will help you too.

- Contact a helpline if you feel you need advice or encouragement. There's a wide range of support groups offering free help and advice (see Further Sources of Information, page 153).

- Try to trust your instincts. Often your gut feeling about a situation will prove to be the right response.

SUMMARY OF CHAPTER 1

Becoming a great mum takes time and experience and, although you can't have a practice run, you can be prepared. Start with these guiding principles:

- Love your child without strings.
- Talk to your child openly and honestly.
- Value the time you spend together.
- Keep your child fit and well.
- Nurture your child's skills and abilities.
- Set a good example.

CHAPTER 2

Your Expectations

From the moment you discover you're pregnant, you are bound to imagine your life as a mum. You'll be patient and understanding; your child will be bright, funny, easy-going and beautiful. And, unlike your friends who are parents, you won't let her have sweets, play on the computer for hours or keep you awake at night.

Expectations, when they are realistic, can be empowering. When you are struggling in the last stages of labour, imagining yourself cuddling your beautiful newborn baby can give you that extra ounce of energy and motivation you need to deliver her safely into the world.

Unrealistic expectations, however, can be devastating, and many pregnant women find it hard to be objective about parenthood. Many imagine life will carry on pretty much as before just with an extra, albeit much wanted, little person to fit into the equation. This is not surprising, of course, because you have no way of knowing exactly what the impact of the new arrival will be. People may tell you it won't be that straightforward – but it doesn't make a lot of sense until you experience it.

'Before getting pregnant I used to imagine life as a mum would be like it is for those celebrity mums you see in so many magazines nowadays – swanning around with my cute baby, stylish clothes and devoted husband. Now I have a six-month-old I'm a little wiser! Yes, my husband is devoted to us both, but do we get any spare time to swan around in stylish clothes together? Never!'

Jacintha, mum to Douglas, aged six months

The truth is, of course, that having children changes everything, from your relationship and your wardrobe, to your job and your sense of self. Life can never be the same again. And while, once you have your baby in your arms, you wouldn't choose to have it any other way, if there's a huge gap between your expectations and the reality of parenthood, coping with the challenges that lie ahead will be that much tougher.

Preparing for parenthood

Thinking through your expectations of life as a family is good for everyone: yourself, your partner and your future child. Try to be realistic about what parenthood involves, remember that your partner's feelings are important too, and give some thought also as to your wishes for your child-to-be.

Stay open-minded and flexible

Having set ideas on any aspect of parenthood can leave you with a whole range of unhelpful emotions such as guilt and disappointment if things don't work out as you planned. Perhaps, for example, you won't be able to have a 'natural' birth; you might have a girl when you'd hoped for a boy; circumstances could mean you have to live in the city when you'd always imagined your children growing up in the country. Having an open, flexible attitude to the life that lies ahead of you will help you deal with the unexpected.

Be ready for the rough as well as the smooth

Becoming a parent will be one of the most fulfilling things you ever do, but often it will also be hard work (especially in the early years), boring (endless nappies to change, meals to cook) and frustrating (little time for yourself, your partner, your friends). Recognising that these emotional and practical challenges exist will help you cope, as will lots of love, help from relatives and friends, good advice and common sense.

Don't make assumptions about your partner's feelings

You might have your own ideas about how you'll manage family life – including household responsibilities, going back to or giving up work and other big issues like discipline, education and money. But you can't assume your partner will feel the same way. Try to look ahead and talk through these issues in advance. This will give you both the chance to settle differences of opinion and work out ways of handling potential areas of conflict before disappointment and resentment set in.

Think about your hopes for your child

Like most parents, you'll want your child to have a great education, lots of opportunities and eventually a good career and lifestyle. But try not to get carried away by your hopes and dreams. Remember that it's one thing to nurture your child's ambition but another to thrust your own ambitions on to her. Rather than piling on the pressure, you need to see your child as unique and special in her own way, and love her first and foremost for who she is, not who you'd like her to be.

'I've always loved music, and when I was pregnant I used to imagine myself and my son sitting at the piano playing duets together. Sadly, he really isn't interested. But although he can't play he does love listening to me playing his favourite songs, so we can still have fun together.'

Aisha, mum to Seb, aged nine

SUMMARY OF CHAPTER 2

Plan for parenthood by thinking ahead about the reality of family life.

- Things don't always work out as you imagine, so stay open-minded and flexible.
- Don't stick your head in the sand. Life as a mum can be incredibly fulfilling, but there will be lots of tough times too.
- Remember it's a joint effort with your partner. Try to talk about the big issues before they come up, and sort out any differences of opinion early on.
- Be realistic about the future for your child. Unreasonable expectations could damage her self-esteem and confidence.

CHAPTER 3

Pregnancy – Caring for Yourself and Your Baby

You're pregnant. You've created a new life. Thousands of women do this every day, but it's still an amazing achievement. And although right now your unborn baby might just be a tiny speck, he's growing fast and is dependent on you for everything. So once you've got over the shock, excitement, relief or panic, you'll want to know how best to make sure the pregnancy goes smoothly and your baby is delivered safe and healthy.

Sorting out your antenatal care

It is possible, with home pregnancy testing, to know that you're having a baby from around six weeks onwards. But like lots of women, while you might feel like shouting out your news from the rooftop, you may decide to keep the news quiet until the risk of miscarriage has significantly dropped, which is around 12 weeks.

There are, however, many good reasons to book in with your midwife and/or GP earlier rather than later. Research has shown that when it comes to delivering a healthy baby, supportive antenatal care is one of the most important factors. And the sooner you sort out your antenatal care, the longer you have to form a good relationship with your caregiver; ask for and use all the advice you need on how to care for yourself (and therefore your baby) and also find out which antenatal tests are available (see page 23) – some of which can take place from 11 weeks.

As your pregnancy progresses, you'll also want to talk through your hopes and wishes for labour and delivery. Although your main concern will be that your baby is born safe and well, your experience during labour and delivery can have an impact on those first few days – and sometimes longer – after you have given birth. The more time you allow yourself to mull over the various options, the better informed you will be and more likely to make the decision that is right for you.

You'll also need to think about where you want to have your baby as this can make a big difference to your confidence on the day. Most babies are born in hospital, although there is an increasing number of birth centres opening across the country. A home birth is also an option. Many women find the hospital environment reassuring, especially if it is their first baby and they don't know what to expect. Others, however, find it stressful, and may prefer to be in the comfort of their own home.

Deciding where to have your baby

- **In a birth centre.** These offer a 'low-tech' environment run by midwives, where the focus is on helping women to use their own resources to cope with labour and birth. There is one-to-one care during labour, there is often a birth pool, and gas and air can be supplied for pain relief. Epidurals are not available. If problems arise and an assisted delivery, caesarean or special baby-care unit is required, you would have to be transferred to hospital by ambulance. Most birth centres are part of the NHS and, while they are not an option in some areas, there are new ones opening all the time.

- **In hospital.** Most babies are born in hospital, and the maternity unit will usually offer all varieties of pain relief, including epidurals, as well as special baby-care units. You may have a choice of which hospital to go to, and many have open evenings giving you the chance to have a look around the delivery rooms and wards. If you opt for a hospital birth, you will be given 'shared care' – this means you are looked after jointly by your GP and a midwife or team of midwives, alternating between your GP and midwife for check-ups and going in to hospital for your ultrasound scans.

- **At home.** A very small number of women choose to have their baby at home. If you choose this option within the NHS you will be assigned to a small team of midwives who will continue with your care after the delivery. You don't need anything special – your midwife will supply you with a home-birth pack (which includes gas and air for pain relief) that contains everything you need. Booking in for a home birth doesn't mean you will inevitably end up having your baby at home. If health concerns arise during your pregnancy, or if during labour there is cause for concern, you may need to transfer to the hospital. You may also decide you want to move to hospital yourself during labour if you need more pain relief than is available at home.

> *'I loved the idea of a home birth – but this was my first baby and I was too nervous to actually opt for one. Zanthe was born at our local hospital, which was fine, but as I managed without an epidural, I'll definitely decide to opt for a home birth next time.'*
>
> Jill, 30, mum to Zanthe, now 11 months

Staying healthy

If you haven't managed to kick the habit already, now's the time to stop smoking, as it increases the risk of stillbirth, low birth weight and pregnancy complications such as miscarriage and bleeding. If you need help quitting, talk to your midwife or GP, or contact the NHS Smoking in Pregnancy helpline (see Further Sources of Information, page 153) for local support.

Similarly, if you are used to skipping meals, getting by on fast food and keeping yourself on the go with mugs of tea or coffee, now's the time to re-examine your fridge habits and focus on eating healthily. Your unborn baby depends on you for all his nutrients, so if you're following a healthy, well-balanced diet, he'll benefit too.

The basic rules are simple. Try to eat a wide variety of different wholesome foods every day: plenty of carbohydrates, five portions of fruit and vegetables a day, and moderate amounts of meat and fish. Tinned or fresh sardines, mackerel and salmon are especially beneficial as they contain essential fatty acids (EFAs) vital for brain development (although some oily fish should be avoided – see page 19).

Dairy products are important for building healthy bones. Try to drink at least one cup of milk a day.

If you are vegetarian you'll need to include pulses, lentils and soya protein as well as fruit and vegetables to make sure you are getting sufficient proteins and minerals. You may also need iron and vitamin B supplements; ask your midwife or GP for advice.

All pregnant women are advised to take a daily supplement of 400mcg folic acid from the time of conception through the first three months of pregnancy to help prevent spina bifida and other neural tube defects in babies.

And don't imagine your pregnancy is a great excuse to pile up the food on your plate. Pregnancy experts advise that most women don't need to increase their calorie intake at all in the first six months and, after that, only by 200 calories a day – the equivalent to just one portion of cheese on toast. In fact, being overweight, or seriously underweight, during pregnancy may increase your risk of complications, including high blood pressure and premature birth.

What to cut down on and avoid

While most foods are beneficial to your unborn baby's health, the following may cause food poisoning or carry other risks.

- Unpasteurised dairy products (especially soft and blue-veined cheeses).

- Undercooked eggs and poultry.

- Home-made mayonnaise (shop-bought made from pasteurised egg is safe).

- Offal and offal-based products, especially liver which though full of iron contains too much vitamin A.

- Undercooked meats and pâtés.

- Pre-prepared meals unless heated thoroughly.

- Unwashed vegetables and pre-washed salads. These should be washed thoroughly as they may carry the toxoplasmosis parasite.

- Certain oily fish such as shark, swordfish and marlin which tend to contain high levels of mercury alcohol and may affect the developing nervous system of a baby. Tinned tuna should be restricted to 140g per week.

- Raw shellfish is best avoided.

- Alcohol: while there is no evidence to show that small amounts of alcohol have an effect on a developing baby, research has shown that frequent (more than two units a day), heavy or binge drinking does. Consequently most women follow the safest course and avoid alcohol during pregnancy.

- Peanuts, if anyone in your family has a nut allergy.

- Caffeine: restrict coffee intake to around 300mg a day (three 100mg cups of instant coffee). Bear in mind that hot chocolate also contains caffeine.

> *'Morning sickness makes eating a real chore. I've found I can only stomach food in small quantities, so now I have five or six mini meals each day instead of three big ones.'*
>
> Sarah, 29, nearly three months pregnant

Sleeping well

Making sure you get a good night's sleep is vital. Sleep boosts the immune system and reduces your chance of falling ill. A weakened immune system could put both you and your baby at risk.

In the early months you'll probably be unable to keep your eyes open. The first trimester when so many vital changes are taking place can be especially tiring. As your baby grows, however, getting to sleep can become a struggle. Trying to get comfortable, worrying about the future and needing a pee can all make sleep elusive. Listen to your body and try to organise your day so that you can rest as much as possible.

Happily, by the middle of the second trimester, most women are full of energy again.

Sleep tips

- Establish a regular, relaxing bedtime routine. Always going to bed and getting up at the same times can help regulate your body clock and make sleep easier to achieve.

- Get comfortable. Invest in a variety of different-shaped pillows to support your tummy and back in bed.

- Take regular exercise (see page 21) to help you sleep more soundly at night, but allow yourself at least three to four hours after exercise to unwind before trying to sleep.

- Teach yourself to catnap. A 30- to 60-minute snooze during the day can really boost your energy levels, and developing the knack of napping is especially useful for coping with sleepless nights once your baby is born.

- Try some relaxation techniques. Yoga, gentle stretching exercises, massage and deep breathing can all help to calm your mind and relax your body ready for sleep.

- Avoid eating or drinking too close to bedtime. Give your body time to digest meals. Heartburn and trips to the loo can interfere with a good night's sleep.

'Once I was about six months pregnant I found I could only get comfortable in bed with a wedged-shaped pillow supporting my tummy. It was invaluable.'

Martine, 32, mum to Samantha, aged three months

Managing your mood changes

Every mum-to-be says that being pregnant is like being on an emotional roller coaster. One minute you feel fine, the next you want to hide your head under a pillow and have a good cry. Mood swings in pregnancy are normal. This is partly due to changing levels of the hormones progesterone and oestrogen. But expecting a baby can also bring lots of natural concerns about the future. Worrying about relationships, money and your baby's health can all have an impact.

Feeling moody is most common in the first trimester. Later, as your body adapts to the changes and you get used to being pregnant, any mood swings should lessen.

If, however, you can't shake off your moodiness, seek help from your GP or midwife. Research has shown that excessive stress can affect your unborn baby, slowing growth and increasing the risk of hyperactivity. It has also been linked to premature birth.

Coping with moodiness

- Talk about it. Discussing your feelings with your partner, friends, family, GP or midwife rather than bottling them up will help to put them into perspective.

- Treat yourself. Doing something that makes you feel good can help you to deal with the lows of pregnancy. Try having a nap, taking a walk or going out with a friend.

- Take regular exercise (see below). Physical activity can raise levels of serotonin, a brain chemical linked to feeling good.

'I must have been a pain a to live with. I was an emotional mess for the first few months, even though we'd been desperate to have a baby. Thankfully my husband was incredibly patient and refused to be shut out. Talking definitely helped.'

Jo, 37, mum to Alex, aged one year

Taking regular exercise

Getting out for a brisk walk, a swim at your local pool or joining a yoga class can have lots of benefits for you and your baby. Regular exercise will boost your energy levels, help you cope with tiredness and build muscle tone and strength, helping you carry the weight you gain during pregnancy. You'll feel happier, sleep better and gradually build up the stamina you need to get you through labour.

Some sports are obviously better avoided during pregnancy, such as high-impact aerobics, contact sports and sports like horse riding where safety can be an issue. Check with your midwife or GP if you are unsure about your preferred choice of exercise and stop when your body tells you to.

Which exercise?

- Swimming is great all-round exercise and especially useful in late pregnancy as the water takes some of your weight.

- Walking is simple to fit into your daily routine, and towards the end of pregnancy can help position the baby ready for birth.

- Yoga is good for increasing flexibility and learning breathing and concentration techniques that are useful during labour.

- Pelvic floor exercises are a must. A good tip is to do a batch every time you wash your hands after going to the loo or while you're travelling to and from work. Despite what you think, no one will know what you're up to.

> *'I've always run, and for the first few months of pregnancy continued with my daily jog. Now I'm five months pregnant and find fast walking more comfortable.'*
>
> Phillipa, 34

Staying safe at work

Managing a job and pregnancy can be quite a challenge. On the one hand you're distracted by the huge change taking place in your life; on the other you may want to prove that you are just as committed to work as ever. For you and your baby's sake, however, pregnancy isn't the time to up the ante. Instead you need to listen to your body and try to establish a sensible balance that's right for you and your baby.

It's also worth knowing that employers have a legal obligation to make sure that work doesn't endanger the health of you or your baby. For example, you have a right to take paid time off for antenatal appointments, regardless of your length of service, and night work can be avoided with a medical certificate from your doctor.

Other specific conditions that can cause problems if you are pregnant are working with animals, radiation, biological agents or certain metals and chemicals. Always tell your employer as soon as you know that you are pregnant so steps can be taken to avoid unnecessary risk.

Your working environment

● Take care of your back. If your job involves sitting at a desk all day, make sure your chair is the right height and provides good lower back support. You may need to use extra cushions.

● Move your feet frequently to help keep the blood circulating.

● Drink plenty of water. Air conditioning in offices can make you feel dehydrated.

● Go for a walk around the office every couple of hours to help keep your circulation active and to re-energise yourself.

● Ask to adjust your hours to avoid the rush hour. Travelling in heavy traffic or crowded public transport can be exhausting.

'Fighting the crowds to get to work every day is a nightmare – especially as I'm quite shy and hate asking for a seat on the tube. Luckily my employer is very sympathetic, and allows me to work from home one day a week.'

Jenine, 27, five and a half months pregnant

Considering antenatal testing

Although certain tests, such as an ultrasound scan, are now the norm, the decision whether or not to have them is still yours. They are usually offered to give you an indication as to how the pregnancy is progressing, and whether your baby is developing normally or has a chromosomal problem such as Down's syndrome or other major problems.

Screening tests indicate the risk of your baby having a specific problem. Diagnostic tests will tell you *for certain* whether or not there is a problem. It's important to bear in mind that diagnostic tests are invasive and therefore carry a slight risk of miscarriage.

Most women who have screening or testing choose to do so because they want to be reassured that everything is fine. And in most cases, everything is fine. But it makes sense when deciding whether or not to go ahead with antenatal testing, to think beforehand about what course of action you would take if you were given bad news.

Booking up antenatal classes

Many women prefer not to think too hard about the fine detail of labour and delivery before they have to, but being properly informed will help you cope better on the day. Antenatal classes provide a great opportunity to find out more, to discuss ideas and worries and to meet other women in your area who are in a similar situation.

Popular classes get booked up early so, if you are keen to take an antenatal course, ask your midwife early on for details of classes nearby. Types of classes vary. You may be able to opt for women-only or couples classes, hospital-based or home-based (such as the NCT – National Childbirth Trust) classes that focus on providing information and practical skills for new parents, or active birth classes based on yoga, and exercises to help with labour and birth.

Choosing a class

● What will be covered? If you want to practise breathing and birthing positions then an active birth class may be more suitable than a parenting skills class.

● How big is the class? Smaller classes may be more friendly but you will be expected to join in more than with a larger class.

● Is there postnatal support? Knowing a group of women who have babies the same age as yours can be very helpful and reassuring.

Bonding with your unborn baby

Bonding can start from the moment you know you are pregnant, although often it's not until you have your first scan or feel your baby move for the first time that you start to feel really attached. Towards the end of your pregnancy, giving yourself time and space to tune into your baby and feel close to him before he is even in your arms will help you to feel positive and motivated during your labour and birth.

Ways to bond

- Try to indulge yourself, especially in the last few weeks, by spending half an hour or so each day relaxing and focusing on your baby.

- Stroke your bump and try to figure out how your baby is lying. As he gets bigger towards the end of your pregnancy, you may be able to identify his bottom, arm or leg as he presses against your tummy.

- Talk to your baby. Babies can hear through the womb from 19–22 weeks' gestation and can recognise your voice and distinguish it from other people's voices from birth onwards.

> *'I talk to my baby when I'm relaxing in a deep bath. I tell him how excited I am about meeting him for the very first time!'*
>
> Catherine, 29, eight and a half months pregnant

SUMMARY OF CHAPTER 3

Caring for your health and well-being over the next nine months will help to give your baby the best start in life.

- Sort out your antenatal care earlier rather than later.
- Eat a well-balanced diet, with a wide variety of fresh, wholesome food.
- Sort out sleep problems to avoid excessive tiredness.
- Feeling moody? Talk about it with your partner, a friend, your midwife or your GP.
- Take some form of regular exercise.
- Stay safe at work. Tell your employer earlier rather than later that you are pregnant and try to listen to your body.
- Remember that the decision whether or not to have antenatal testing is yours.
- Join an antenatal class. You'll be given lots of relevant information and may make new friends too.
- Bond with your baby. You'll be meeting him soon, and feeling close will help to motivate you during the birth.

Chapter 4

Birth – What to Expect

As your delivery date approaches, you'll feel incredible surges of excitement. Any day now this tiny person you have been nurturing for the past nine months will be in your arms.

Getting to this point, however, involves an incredible journey into the unknown. What will labour really be like? Will you be able to manage the pain? What happens if the birth doesn't go to plan?

No one can answer all these questions. But there's plenty you can do to prepare in advance. Looking after yourself in the days running up to labour, for example, and knowing what to expect on the day itself, will give you the best chance of having a smooth and safe delivery – and an incredible experience, too.

Genning up on birth procedures

Your antenatal classes (see Chapter 3, page 24) will provide lots of useful information, and you can discuss the options that are available at the birth centre or hospital where you are having your baby, and the kind of birth experience you would like with your caregiver (your midwife or GP).

Whatever your birth plans, unforeseen events may mean you need some medical help during labour to bring your baby safely into the world. These range from foetal monitoring, episiotomies (a surgical cut to help the baby emerge from the vagina) and assisted delivery (the use of medical instruments such as forceps or a ventouse vacuum cup) to induction (artificial stimulation of labour) and caesarean.

Whatever your ideal scenario, it makes sense to stay open-minded. In the weeks to come, when you're feeling shattered and your hormones are in free fall, you don't also want to be coping with feelings of disappointment because the birth didn't go as you'd hoped.

The most important outcome is that both you and your baby emerge safe and well. And whatever it takes, when you have delivered your baby and can hold her in your arms, you deserve to feel incredibly proud.

Choosing your birth partner

Whether it's your partner, sister, mum or best friend, research has shown that having someone as well as a midwife with you during labour really makes a difference, from reducing the need for pain relief to decreasing the likelihood of assisted delivery. If, for example, you're exhausted and feel like you'd rather do anything than give birth, just hearing someone you care about telling you how brilliantly you are doing can give you that extra spurt of desperately needed willpower.

Your birth partner can also liaise between you and your midwife, calling for help, for example, when you feel like you need to push, or discussing other pain relief if you are in need of something more. They can also help by encouraging you to keep mobile; massaging your back to help ease the pain of contractions; enabling you to change your position; giving you drinks and small snacks to keep you properly hydrated and energised; assisting you to get in and out of the bath, shower or birthing pool and offering cool flannels or a face spray.

Most couples want to be together for the birth of their child, but whoever you choose as your birth partner, it's wise for them to gen up on the birth experience too, so they also know what to expect on the day.

> *'I was pretty anxious throughout Jennie's labour and the birth. Seeing her in so much pain was upsetting, and I was worrying about the baby too. Given the choice, though, I wouldn't have missed it for the world.'*
>
> Steven, 35, dad to Jack, aged four months

Writing your birth plan

Doing this will not only help you to focus on the birth but will also help you to make decisions on how, for example, you plan to cope with contractions. Talk with your midwife and/or GP when you are thinking about your birth plan. Working with them is the best way to get what you want as their aim is to help you make informed and realistic choices, depending on your personal circumstances, and to support those choices. And don't forget to discuss your wishes with your birth partner too, as on the day he or she will be the one helping you to make your wishes known.

Some hospitals offer pre-prepared birth plans with tick boxes for you to fill in. You can add to it if necessary or just write your own. Bear in mind, however, that this is a 'wish list' – you can, and may need to, change your mind at any time, even during labour, as circumstances may arise which you won't have been able to plan for.

Give one copy of your birth plan to your midwife on the day, and keep one for yourself and your birth partner.

Details you may wish to cover include the following issues:

- **Birth partner.** Who do you want to be with you?

- **Monitoring.** Are you happy to have your baby monitored?

- **Pain relief.** Are you planning to concentrate on self-help techniques such as massage and breathing? Will you be using a TENS machine? Are you happy to have pethidine or do you definitely not want it? Are you planning an epidural?

- **Caesarean.** If you need one, do you want an epidural, if possible, so you can be awake when your baby is born?

- **Episiotomy.** Would you rather tear than be cut?

- **Vitamin K** (more important for babies who are pre-term, small or have had a difficult birth). Would you like your baby to have an injected or oral dose?

- **Third stage** (delivery of the placenta). Do you want this to happen naturally or would you prefer an injection to speed up the process?

Practising breathing exercises and relaxation

Staying as calm and relaxed as possible during labour and birth can have a powerful effect on pain and stress levels. Whether you've decided to try for an active birth or not, learning to breathe in a full and relaxed way is an incredibly useful weapon against stress and pain. This is because when you are tense or anxious, your breathing will become shallow and more rapid, which in turn causes the body to receive less oxygen, so raising stress levels. If you are able to focus on your breathing (exhaling and inhaling deeply and calmly) you can reverse this process.

Your antenatal classes may well focus to some extent on breathing and relaxation techniques, but it's not complicated and you can practise at home too.

- Sit comfortably with your back straight and relax your chin towards your chest.

- Place your hands on your lower abdomen so you can feel the rhythm of each in and out breath.

- Exhale slowly through your mouth so that each breath is long and smooth and your lungs are completely empty.

- Rest, then spontaneously breathe in, but this time through your nose, allowing your abdomen to expand.

- Continue like this, breathing slowly and calmly so one breath flows naturally into the next.

Getting your baby into a good position

Sometimes the difference between a smooth labour and a difficult labour depends simply on how well the baby is positioned. If your baby has the back of her head and spine against your spine, labour may be slower, cause more backache and increase the need for an assisted delivery. On the other hand, if your baby is anterior (positioned with her spine to the front of the uterus) labour will be quicker and easier.

Most babies engage (move down into the pelvis) from around 36 weeks so before this happens it's a good idea to try to help yours settle into an anterior position. The idea is to try to keep your pelvis tipped forward as much as possible. When the pelvis is tipped back, the heaviest part of the baby (the head and spine) tends to swing round to your back too.

- Try to sit with your pelvis tilted forward whenever you can. Your knees should be lower than your hips. Push a cushion under your bottom to help.

- Punctuate spells of sitting by getting up and walking about every half an hour (our pelvis naturally tips forward when we are upright).

- If you're really keen, try watching television on all fours with your bottom in the air. This will help to move your baby forward in your pelvis.

Conserving your energy

Many women feel they have to get their whole house in order before their baby is born, and in the last few weeks of pregnancy decide to redecorate the bathroom or clean out the garage. Nesting is considered by some as a sure sign that your baby will be born soon.

Try to resist the urge to do too much. Giving birth can be very tiring and the more reserves you have in store, the better you'll cope. And, after all, your baby won't care whether there is dust under the beds or unwanted junk in the attic, but having a mother who has enough energy to help bring her safely into the world will be appreciated.

Slow down and use these last few pre-baby weeks wisely.

- Meet up with friends, go to the cinema or visit the theatre while you still can.

- Treat yourself to a haircut, a manicure or a pedicure. It may be a while before you have a chance to pamper yourself again.

- If you feel the need to nest, focus on worthwhile activities. Stock up the freezer with easy meals, or check you have plenty of supplies of toiletries.

● Rest as much as possible. You'll soon have months of sleep deficiency so top up now with lots of lie-ins and afternoon naps.

Managing labour

As your due date approaches (and, in many cases, comes and goes) you'll be noting every tweak and twinge, trying to decide whether or not labour has started. Staying calm and feeling rested will make all the difference once real labour kicks in, so it's worth being certain that you really are in labour before heading for hospital or calling your midwife.

Many couples worry that they won't recognise the signs of labour and will end up with an unplanned home birth or a last-minute dash to the delivery ward. But it's far more common to have a false alarm, arrive far too early and spend valuable resting time travelling backwards and forwards between hospital and home.

A first labour can last up to 12 hours or more, so it makes sense to spend as much of this time as possible at home, conserving energy. At home you can walk around, distract yourself, make as much noise as you like, have small snacks and drinks, and lie down when you wish. Once, however, your contractions are five minutes apart or closer, or if you need help with the pain, or your waters have broken or you are bleeding, you should make the move.

The first stage of labour

During the first stage of labour, the cervix is opening up to allow the baby's head through the birth canal. Contractions are the muscles of the uterus thinning and pulling back the cervix. This stage is usually the longest. Your goal is to try to help labour progress smoothly.

● The power of contractions can be quite overwhelming and you may feel scared at times. Don't be afraid to ask for support or pain relief if you need it.

● Try to stay upright as this allows the baby's head to press on the cervix, making contractions more effective.

- Rotate your hips or walk around between contractions to help ease the pain.

- Use your breathing techniques to breathe through the pain. As the contraction begins, concentrate on exhalation and releasing tension with the breath. Rest, then allow the inhalation to begin, repeating the cycle through the wave of each contraction.

- Counting through contractions helps too.

The second stage of labour

Once the cervix is fully dilated (10cm) you will move into the second stage of labour. This period is known as transition and can last from a few minutes to an hour or more as you await the compulsion to bear down and push your baby out into the world.

Huge amounts of support are often needed at this stage, especially if you've had a long labour and feel exhausted.

- Get into a good position that feels comfortable and effective. Squatting or kneeling allows the pelvis to open wide and encourages gravity to help you push the baby out. Being upright also helps to reduce pain and shorten labour.

- Listen to your body. Wait until you feel the urge to push and then go with it. If you don't feel the urge, stay calm and try a change of position as this may help.

- Ask to be told when the head becomes visible as this can be really encouraging. Some mothers use a mirror so they can see what is happening. Touching the head yourself will also boost your morale.

The third stage of labour

Once your baby's head is born, the rest of the body usually follows straightaway. You will probably feel an incredible sense of physical relief. Your baby's arrival marks the end of the second stage and the beginning of the third – the delivery of the placenta. This may be left to occur naturally or, depending on your wishes, be aided by an injection.

Meeting your baby

If your labour and delivery were straightforward, the midwife will hand you your baby straightaway to hold. Newborn babies can look rather strange – a bit squashed, maybe covered in vernix (the greasy cream-like substance that coated the skin in the womb) and even a bit bloody. Chances are, however, you won't even notice and instead will feel a flood of intense emotion and incredible elation as you hold this little person you have waited so long to meet.

If the labour was difficult or very fast, however, or your baby needs special care, you may feel dazed, overwhelmed and even frightened. These reactions are normal. Some women fall in love with their babies at first sight but, for others, love needs to grow slowly. However you feel at that first meeting, remind yourself what you've been through and allow yourself some sympathy and understanding. For now, your baby will be happy just to smell your skin, feel your warmth and hear your voice.

If you'd like to, and you feel up to it, letting your baby suckle on your breast will be immensely comforting for her and incredibly rewarding for you. Also, the clear, golden-yellow fluid (colostrum) which your breasts will produce before your milk comes in, will help start your baby's digestive system working, and protect against infection.

SUMMARY OF CHAPTER 4

Being properly prepared for the birth can increase your chances of having a smooth delivery.

- Find out all you can about the birth and what to expect from antenatal classes, your GP or midwife, friends and family.
- Make sure your birth partner knows what to expect too.
- Write a birth plan, but remember this is a best-case scenario and that things don't always go to plan.
- Prepare yourself physically. Practise breathing exercises, try to get your baby into a good position for birth and take plenty of rest.

When labour starts:

- Don't rush to hospital too soon.
- Expect labour to be long and tiring.
- Listen to your body. Whatever you wrote in your birth plan, remember that you can change your mind at any time.

When you meet your baby for the first time:

- Try not to be shocked by your baby's appearance.
- Don't worry if you're not overwhelmed by feelings of joy and elation; love sometimes takes time to grow.
- Try to suckle your baby as colostrum (the first milk) is nutritionally valuable.

CHAPTER 5

Life as a New Mum – the First Two Weeks

Your first few days and weeks at home with your new baby is a unique and, in many ways, challenging time. Hopefully, you are enormously happy, enchanted by this tiny life you and your partner have created, and excited by the new life that stretches ahead.

At the same time you're exhausted, unable to think beyond the next feed, coping with fluctuating hormones, and wondering whether life will ever feel 'normal' again.

Getting your new family off to the best possible start begins with looking after yourself. Your body has been through a huge physical challenge and now you have to deal with sleepless nights as well. Eating properly, resting and getting as much sleep as possible will help to give you the emotional and physical resources you need to cope while caring for your new baby. Although, as you hold him in your arms, you may wonder how you will manage, it's helpful to know that newborn babies are much sturdier than you might think, and as you get to know him over the next few days and weeks, so your confidence will grow.

'Looking back, those first few weeks at home with Jasmine were really surreal. Half the time I didn't know if it was night or day. I rarely managed to change out of my nightdress! But I remember it as a really special time as well – just myself, my partner and our new baby.'

Lizzie, mum to Jasmine, aged six months

Caring for yourself

Whatever type of birth you had, you are bound to feel delicate for a while. Even if you haven't had stitches you'll feel tender and sore, and going to the loo may be uncomfortable. As your uterus contracts and decreases in size you may have after-pains, and you will bleed for two to three weeks as the uterus sheds its lining. Around day three, when your milk comes in, your breasts will feel swollen and heavy.

If your baby was born by caesarean section you'll be in hospital for four or five days and then it will take another six weeks or so before you feel fully fit again. Bear in mind that you've had major abdominal surgery and your recovery will be slower than that of mums who've had a vaginal delivery.

Once you are home your midwife will visit you for the first ten days to check that you are recovering as expected, to make sure that your baby is doing well and to help you with feeding and everyday baby care. If you have any worries about your health (heavy bleeding, unusual discharge, chest pains, difficulty going to the loo, swollen legs or a temperature) call your midwife, even if she has already visited that day.

Try to take the first few days slowly. Stay in bed as much as you can, let family and friends do the running around, and concentrate on getting better while getting to know your baby.

Understanding your emotions

Don't be surprised if your initial feelings of blissful contentment vanish after two or three days, leaving you tearful and confused. Just as your milk comes in, so your hormones take a huge dip, and suddenly everything from changing a nappy to making a cup of tea can become a challenge. Often referred to as 'baby blues', these feelings are unsettling but perfectly normal. Be kind to yourself, snuggle down with your baby and let those around you make that cup of tea!

● Ask for help from your midwife. Besides checking your physical recovery, she'll be able to answer your questions and reassure you that every new mum feels the same around this time, and that as your body settles down, so will your emotions.

- Don't expect too much of yourself. Worrying about dust or laundry duties will only increase your sense of being overwhelmed, so be firm with yourself and cut down your 'to do' list – it's just you and your baby who need attention right now.

- If necessary, debrief the birth. Many new mums feel the need to go over the details of their labour and delivery, especially if it didn't go as expected. Your midwife can explain things you don't understand, or you can ask to see your obstetrician. Even talking it through with a willing friend or your antenatal teacher can help.

'My first night at home was a nightmare. Cora cried and cried, and I hadn't a clue how to comfort her. By the time my midwife arrived the next morning I was sobbing as well. But she quickly sorted us out and told me I could phone her any time when I needed help.'

Gill, mum to Cora, aged three

Eating well

Lots of new mums feel really hungry after giving birth, as labour uses a phenomenal number of calories. Eating well will help get your energy levels back to normal so you can care for your baby. Of course, you won't be up to going round the supermarket for a few days at least. But if you were able to get organised before the birth, your freezer and food cupboard will already be stocked with food that just needs warming up – lasagne, casseroles, pasta sauces. If not, don't forget that most supermarkets now take orders over the phone or internet and will deliver to your home. And although it costs a little more, now's a good time to treat yourself.

- Continue the healthy diet you started while you were pregnant, concentrating on lots of wholegrain cereals, fresh fruit and vegetables, and plenty of protein, calcium and iron.

- If you are breastfeeding you'll need around an extra 300 calories a day, plus lots of fluid (about 8–12 glasses) to help keep up your milk supply.

- If you weren't able to stock up the freezer with ready meals before your baby was born, ask any visitors coming to see your baby not to bring flowers but a home-made meal instead!

- When you feel peckish opt for nutritious snacks such as yoghurt, a bowl of muesli, a wholemeal sandwich or a baked potato.

Starting exercise

Gentle daily exercises will relieve your tiredness so you can cope better with your baby's needs. It will also help you to get back into shape. Get started on pelvic floor exercises as soon as you can bear to. Not only do they improve circulation which aids healing, they also cut the risk of stress incontinence, and will make a big difference to your sex life. Meanwhile ask your midwife for suggestions and guidance on gentle exercises you can do at home over the next couple of weeks.

Vigorous exercise, however, should be avoided until bleeding has stopped, and if you've had a caesarean you will be advised to wait until after your six-week check before doing any exercise, apart from pelvic floor lifts.

Getting enough rest

Dealing with broken nights is one of the hardest adjustments you'll have to make now you have a baby. In these early days your baby will need feeding every few hours and at times you may feel like the waking dead, barely able to hold a conversation. It helps to know that this stage won't last forever – there will come a time when your baby settles into a more predictable routine and sleeps for longer between feeds. Meanwhile, don't feel guilty about having afternoon naps. Getting enough rest is important for you and your baby, otherwise you run the risk of poor milk production if you are breastfeeding, postnatal depression, and a lowered immune system.

- Sleep when your baby sleeps. It's really tempting to catch up on chores or make phone calls when your baby is safely in the land of nod, but napping when your baby naps is the best way of boosting your sleep quota.

- If you can't sleep, try to unwind. Just resting in the bath or lazing on the sofa with a book will help to conserve your energy.

- Make a pact with your partner and take it in turns to have lie-ins at the weekend. Knowing you'll be able to catch up once a week will help you to deal with tiredness the rest of the time.

- Keep a check on visitors. Naturally, friends and family will want to visit, and you'll be keen for them to meet your new baby, but having visitors in the house can be tiring. If you're not up to it, reschedule – after all, there's still plenty of time for celebrations.

'Everyone tells you to take it easy when you've just had a baby – but it's really hard. I just wanted everything to be perfect – clean sleep suits for the baby, clean sheets for me, food in the fridge and flowers on the table. But tiredness catches up with you. I wish now I had cared less and slept more.'

Sarah, mum to Jacob, aged five months

Caring for your newborn

Amazingly, your newborn's needs are very few. But everything you do for him, from giving him a bath to breastfeeding, is a new experience. Even the simplest tasks can be nerve-wracking when it's your first time.

Helping him feel safe and secure will keep crying to a minimum and boost your confidence. Try, for example, to approach him quietly and slowly, talking to him before you touch him so he knows you are there. And bear in mind that he won't like being cold, wet or naked for too long. So whether you are topping and tailing, changing his nappy or getting him dressed, make sure the room is warm, and that everything you need is to hand, and try to work calmly and quickly.

Feeding

For your baby's health, breast milk is the best possible option. Numerous studies have shown that it contains all the necessary nutrients in exactly the right amounts to nourish a baby for the first six months. It also contains antibodies that protect against common infant infections like gastroenteritis and ear, urinary and respiratory infections. It may also help protect against allergy-related conditions like asthma and eczema, and reduce the risk of childhood diabetes and leukaemia.

A number of studies have also shown that it may boost a baby's intelligence level, perhaps because breast milk contains long-chain polyunsaturated fatty acids, which are essential to brain development.

When it's going well, breastfeeding can be pleasurable and rewarding. The close physical contact helps to develop a strong bond between mother and baby, and for many mothers it provides an incredible sense of achievement.

But breastfeeding isn't the only way to be a great mum. For some women it can be a struggle, and no one should feel they are a failure if breastfeeding doesn't work out. There's no evidence to show that formula-fed babies are any less well loved, and holding your baby close in your arms while you feed him can feel as fulfilling as breastfeeding.

If, however, breastfeeding doesn't appeal to you because you just don't like the idea of it, no one in your family breastfed or you think you couldn't cope, it may be a good idea to talk to your midwife or a breastfeeding counsellor first. While no one should put pressure on you to breastfeed, getting as much information about it as you can before you make up your mind might help, especially as once you've started feeding your baby formula milk, switching to breastfeeding won't be easy.

Although it may be natural to breastfeed, this doesn't mean it always comes naturally. For most mums (and babies) it's a skill that needs to be learnt and practised. Get as much support and advice as you can. Ask your midwife, antenatal teacher, breastfeeding counsellor (see Further Sources of Information, page 153), even other breastfeeding mums for help. And don't lose heart. Although at times you might think this just isn't for you, bear in mind that the more you do it, the easier it gets.

Latching on is the real key to success. If your baby isn't latched on properly he'll make your nipples sore and breastfeeding will quickly become intolerable.

- Start by getting comfortable. You and your baby should be tummy to tummy with his nose opposite your nipple and his head and body in line. Use cushions to support your back and arms, bringing your baby towards you, rather than leaning down towards him.

- Help your baby to latch on by stroking his cheek with your finger so he opens his mouth wide. Move him towards your breast, aiming your nipple at the roof of his mouth. When he has a good mouthful he'll close his mouth, forming a tight seal – he should have all of the nipple and plenty of the areola (pigmented area around the nipple) in his mouth.

- Ease him off. When he's had enough, he may fall asleep and naturally slide off your breast. Otherwise, put the tip of your little finger in the corner of his mouth to break the seal.

'I almost abandoned breastfeeding when I developed a blocked duct – my nipple was so sore and my breast so tender. I contacted a breastfeeding counsellor and she suggested I expressed to keep my milk production going while I healed. I was able to hire an electric pump, which worked wonderfully. Ellie still had plenty of milk, and my breast was able to recover.'

Ruth, mum to Ellie, aged nine months

Sleeping

For the first few weeks, whenever he's not feeding, your new baby will probably be sleeping. On average, newborns sleep for around 16 hours a day, dropping off whenever they need a rest.

Having your baby close to you at night can be very reassuring, and practical as he will need frequent feeding. One solution is to put your baby in a crib or carrycot next to the bed. Alternatively, invest in a cot with a drop-down side that can be placed alongside your bed.

If you choose to have your baby in bed with you, bear in mind the risks: you might roll over in your sleep and suffocate him, or he could get caught between the wall and the bed, or he could roll out of the bed and be injured. Bear in mind too that the same risks apply if you fall asleep with your baby on the sofa or in an armchair. Also, experts warn against sleeping with your baby if you or your partner smoke, have recently drunk alcohol, taken medication or are especially tired.

SIDS

Tiny babies lie so still and breathe so quietly when they are sleeping that it's natural to worry, especially as cot death (also known as SIDS – Sudden Infant Death Syndrome) is the most common cause of death in babies under one. There are, however, clear guidelines available for reducing the risk:

- The safest place for your baby to sleep is in a cot in your room for the first six months.

- Place your baby on his back to sleep, with his feet to the foot of the cot, to prevent wriggling down under the covers.

- Use cotton sheets and blankets, tucking covers in securely.

- Make sure the mattress is firm, easy to clean, dry and well aired.

- Do not let your baby get too hot. Keep his head uncovered, and keep the room temperature constant (around 16–20°C/ 61–68°F).

- Don't let anyone smoke in the same house as your baby.

'In the early days when I was so shattered, I really worried about falling asleep on the sofa while feeding Euan. Putting the TV or radio on helped – sometimes I even set the alarm on my watch to wake me up if I did drop off.'

Jackie, mum to Euan, aged one and a half

Comforting

Crying is distressing to hear but it's perfectly normal. When your baby cries he's just trying to tell you that something isn't right. Crying, at this age, is the only way he can let you know what his needs and feelings are. He'll cry, for example, when he's hungry, tired, lonely, bored, startled, uncomfortable or too hot or cold. On average, babies cry for one to four hours a day, so you'll quickly get used to what his different cries mean, and how best to comfort him.

When your baby cries you'll find it hard to resist. And research has shown that babies whose cries are answered quickly tend to be more secure and strongly attached to their parents than those who are left to 'cry it out'.

A constantly crying baby, however, can exhaust even the most patient parent. There may be times when, besides reminding yourself that your baby isn't crying deliberately to frustrate you, you need to put him safely in his cot and take some time to calm down yourself. It's natural to feel upset when you can't calm your baby, but getting worked up yourself won't ease the situation.

When you can't figure out why your baby is crying, try the following:

● Smiling and talking in a loving and calm voice. Although there will probably be times when you feel tired and irritable, bear in mind that babies can pick up on tension which may make them more fretful.

● Cuddling. You are his favourite person and he may just want to be close to you.

● Swaddling. Newborns can't control their movements easily and once they've started thrashing around may find it hard to stop. Wrapping him firmly in a blanket or sheet may help him to relax and fall asleep.

- Rocking. A rocking motion seems to stimulate special cells in a baby's ears that have a calming effect.

- Letting him suck. Whether it is your finger, his thumb or a dummy (keep this as a last resort), sucking can be very soothing.

- Taking him out. Even if it's dark, a trip outdoors for some fresh air can quickly change a baby's mood.

Bonding

For some new mums, bonding begins as soon as they meet their baby for the first time. For others, feelings of love can take many months to emerge. Perhaps you had a difficult birth, your baby needs special care, he or she isn't the sex you longed for or doesn't look as you imagined. Try to talk about your feelings to your partner, your midwife or a close friend. Sharing your thoughts will help to relieve any sense of shame or guilt.

Occasionally difficulties in bonding may signal postnatal depression. This may be hard to recognise in yourself so it's important to discuss any negative feelings with someone such as your partner, midwife or GP or someone else you feel close to. Getting the right kind of help and support as soon as possible is vital to your recovery.

Taking time to get to know your baby is one of the best ways to help you develop a close and loving relationship.

- Enjoy your baby. There's no rush. These are precious times so relish the day-to-day physical tasks such as dressing, feeding, bathing and changing. Marvelling at his tiny body, stroking him gently, holding him close – all this will help to stimulate your protective feelings, as well as having a wonderfully relaxing effect.

- Touch your baby. Skin-to-skin contact is one of the most powerful ways you can get to know your baby and helps to form a strong emotional bond. Set aside peaceful times (perhaps after feeding) when you can hold your baby against your skin and enjoy a sense of closeness.

- Talk to your baby. Even though he's just been born, your baby will respond to the sound of your voice, turning his head, wiggling or kicking.

- Look at your baby. When you hold him in your arms (20–25cm away) he can focus on your face and make eye contact.

Health

New babies can be a worry, and only time and experience will help you to decide when his health is really a cause for concern. You may, for example, be told to trust your instinct, but it's only when you really get to know your baby that you can develop a gut feeling where your baby's health is concerned.

- If you're worried about your baby, talk to someone – your doctor, midwife or health visitor. However trivial or silly you think the problem might be, the health professionals are there to help so ask for advice when you need it.

- If you think your baby might be unwell run through a checklist of symptoms: Is he alert? Does he respond to noise or other stimuli? Is he still feeding? Are his reflexes normal? If you are unsure don't waste time. Take him to your GP, baby clinic or hospital straightaway.

- Keep a list of emergency numbers by the phone.

SUMMARY OF CHAPTER 5

- Caring for yourself is very important. If you feel well and happy, you'll cope better with your new baby, so eat regular healthy meals, start some gentle exercise to boost your energy levels and get as much rest as possible.
- As you get in tune with your newborn your confidence will grow. Focus on meeting his needs quickly and calmly, and remember:
  - Breastfeeding is a skill that needs to be learnt and practised. The key to success is getting your baby to 'latch on' correctly.
  - When putting your baby to sleep, take steps to cut the risk of SIDS (Sudden Infant Death Syndrome).
  - If you have any concerns about your baby's health, however trivial they may seem, get advice from your GP, midwife or health visitor.

CHAPTER 6

Life as a Family

Now your baby is born you are a real family. And if your family life is happy and stable, your baby will be content and secure too.

Unfortunately, for many relationships the first year after a birth can be among the rockiest. Both you and your partner are shattered and have little time left at the end of the day for each other. There are fewer and fewer occasions when you are alone together – if your baby is not with one of you, she is with the other – and life revolves around her needs, which can't be postponed. Inevitably, with less time to talk and feel close, issues like who empties the bins or gets up in the night for the baby can create conflict. Both of you need more love and attention, but instead resentment may build.

Even tiny babies can pick up on atmospheres, and they react badly to feelings of stress and unhappiness. If you start to grow apart during these early months, it can become increasingly hard to get your relationship back on track in the years that follow. Time and energy invested now will help build a strong and happy family unit that's good for you and your child.

Shared parenting

Not only is shared parenting (taking on equal responsibility for childcare and household tasks) good for parents, it's also good for your baby. You and your partner benefit from both being involved but having some free time too; and your baby benefits from getting the undivided attention of you both.

- Share the day-to-day care of your new baby. Many new dads are so sensitive to criticism or nervous about getting it wrong that they quickly give up. But apart from breastfeeding, your partner can do all the baby chores as well as you can – if he's allowed to practise. If you find it hard to hand over your baby, especially if she starts to cry or becomes fussy, leave the room – or even the house. Your partner needs the space and the time to build his confidence without you watching over his shoulder.

- Split the domestic workload. Even if one of you is out of the house working full time, finding a way to help with household chores at the weekend or in the evenings will prevent resentment building up.

- Try to be practical. There's no point in you both being exhausted at the same time. If your partner is out at work all day, let him sleep at night during the week and take over night feeds at the weekend so that you can rest.

- Go out and spend time together as a family, even if it's just going to your favourite café for a cup of coffee or a stroll around the park. Sharing happy times will increase the incentive for sorting out everyday niggles.

- Talk about it. Most couples can cope with busy working lives, a relationship and the odd spot of housework. But once a baby is on the scene, the extra hours needed for feeding, changing and soothing by parents who are surviving on barely any sleep will take its toll. Understanding how this impacts on each other's lives will help ease the resentment.

Finding time for yourselves

Your baby is a bundle of joy but her demands are non-stop. She wants round-the-clock love and attention, and trying to find time for your partner too can leave you feeling unbearably stretched in all directions. But having a strong relationship is good for you and good for family life. When you and your partner are feeling close and supportive, the stresses and strains of life with a new baby will be easier to handle. So try to find time to be on your own together, without baby in tow.

- Find time for sex. Lack of sleep, low-grade bickering and financial worries can all take their toll, and result in your sex life nosediving. Making love will not only bring you closer, but also help you to relax and feel happier too.

- Timetable a weekly babysitter (or join a babysitting circle) so that you can go out together on a regular basis, even if it's just for an hour or so. Once it's booked in the diary you are less likely to cancel.

- Switching off the television and having a takeaway together will give you the chance to chat without being distracted.

- Ask grandparents to help out. Perhaps they could even care for your baby while you have a night away together. You may find it hard not to worry, but there's no reason to go far from home; the aim is simply to have an uninterrupted night in one another's company.

- Treat yourselves and get someone in to help with ironing and cleaning. Then there's no excuse for not having time to enjoy each other's company.

- Let your partner know how much you appreciate him. Give him the occasional gift, make a loving phone call to his office, even run his bath! Being generous with your love and time will encourage him to be generous with his.

'I knew I was neglecting Simon after Josie was born. I just fell head over heels in love with her, and didn't have any time or energy left for him. It was only when Simon finally confronted me I realised how lonely he was. Now I'm making much more of an effort, which has made us stronger as a family.'

Sharon, mum to Josie, aged nine months

Being a single parent

Whether you've chosen to become a single parent, or have had single parenthood thrust upon you, once your baby is born, yours is still a family like any other. And although coping alone will be at times frightening, there can be positive aspects to being a single parent.

In the early days, for example, you will have only yourself and your baby to worry about. It'll be hard work, but also an incredibly special time as you settle and adapt to each other's rhythms. You will develop a very close relationship with your child, often doing more with her than two parents manage. You won't be torn between keeping your baby and your partner happy. And while you may often wonder how life might have been different for your child with two parents, you can also remind yourself that children are happier if you are happy: no parent would wish their child to be piggy in the middle of a malfunctioning relationship.

The biggest problem for children of single parents is often low income. But even without financial worries, bringing up a baby on your own may at times be frightening, exhausting and lonely. Coping by yourself, for example, with a crying or sick baby, may stretch you to your limit. Being stuck in the house with no one else to talk to will leave you feeling isolated. Planning ahead for difficult times, and trying to stay in control of your life, will help to make it work.

- Build up a good support network. Make a list of everyone you know and how they can help. Include parents, siblings, old friends, new friends, neighbours, health visitor and community services. And imagine who you would contact when you need help – whether it's practical advice, a shoulder to cry on, a lift to the shops or company on holiday. Just knowing there's someone available for you will help ease any sense of loneliness.

- Take good care of yourself. Your baby is relying on you, and the healthier and happier you are, the more love and attention you will be able to give her. Routines are important. Have healthy meals at regular times, take regular exercise (make use of the crèche at your local leisure centre) and get plenty of rest, sleeping when your baby sleeps.

● Try to get out every day with your baby. Making contact with other people, having a change of scene and keeping busy will help to prevent feelings of isolation.

● Have regular time away from your baby. Although having a social life may take some organisation, it will be worth it. Joining a babysitting circle will help keep costs down and going out with friends, going to see a film and having some 'me time' will be incredibly refreshing as well as giving you the space to put any worries or problems into perspective.

● Get involved. Your antenatal group, church or local mother and toddler group are good places to meet people and make friends. As your child gets older the school's parent-teacher association (PTA) often needs extra helpers and is a great way of building friendships.

> *'I adore Oliver, and I've never regretted being a single mum, even though there have been many times when it's been tough. But I am lucky, my family are always there to help out when I'm tired or need a break.'*
>
> Racheal, mum to Zoe, aged two

SUMMARY OF CHAPTER 6

● The first year after birth can be the rockiest time for many relationships.
● Shared parenting helps prevent resentment.
● To keep a strong, happy relationship you need to spend time together.
● Single parenthood has positive aspects but you need to plan ahead and stay in control.

CHAPTER 7

Your Healthy Baby

You can't believe how fast your baby is growing. Within a matter of weeks he has changed from a sleepy newborn to an alert infant, putting on weight, gaining control of his head and, before you know it, practising his first wobbly smile and baby babbles.

Keeping your baby healthy is a priority and one of the biggest responsibilities you have. And while it's inevitable, especially in his first year, that at some stage you'll be calling your GP for help and advice, there are lots of simple ways you can help to keep him fit and strong and give him the best possible start in life.

Introducing a healthy diet

If you've been lucky enough to be able to breastfeed your baby, you've already made a major contribution to his health. And the longer you do it the better. But even if you only managed a few days you can feel pleased with yourself as your baby will have benefited from the colostrum you produce before your milk comes in, which is packed with antibodies to strengthen his immune system.

For the first six months of his life, whether it's breast or bottle, milk is the only food your baby needs. In fact, giving him solids before six months could cause him health problems, especially if you or other family members suffer from allergies like eczema, asthma and hay fever. This is because before six months a baby's kidneys are not mature enough to cope with anything other than milk. The gut is still porous, and proteins (the parts of food that cause allergies) can leak into the bloodstream. If this happens, a baby's immune system reacts the way it would react to an infection, triggering food allergies and respiratory illnesses.

Of course, some babies seem permanently ravenous, turning their head to cast a greedy eye over your sandwich even while they are happily guzzling at the breast. If your baby seems hungrier than normal, and hasn't hit the six-month benchmark yet, it may just be a matter of feeding him more often. Otherwise talk to your health visitor for advice.

Once he hits six months, however, your growing baby will not only be ready for the new tastes that food provides, he'll also need it. Maintaining his incredible growth rate requires plenty of calories, and solid food will give him the extra energy he needs. Also, the stores of iron (vital for healthy growth) are now starting to dwindle, and solid food will supply him with these extra nutrients.

If you are really enjoying breastfeeding, you may resist the idea of starting your baby on solids. Don't worry though, as he's not going to dump you to start a new relationship with your local supermarket quite yet. In fact, milk will be a major source of nutrition throughout his first year. But delaying solids beyond six months can cause problems later on, as teaching older babies to chew can be difficult. Chewing is good because it helps your baby to practise moving his tongue and mouth, ready to learn how to talk.

Tasting solids for the first time is an incredible experience for your baby, and one definitely worth capturing with the camera. But don't take it personally if what goes in comes rolling right back out. His first tastes are more about experiencing something new than gaining extra nourishment. Your aim is to encourage him to enjoy eating, while gently introducing him to an increasing range of foods and textures, and avoiding foods that could compromise his health.

Advice as to which foods are suitable and which foods should be avoided can sometimes change, so check with your health visitor or at your baby clinic. As a general guideline, you'll probably be advised to start with baby rice mixed with milk (breast or formula) to a runny consistency. This will be gentle on his tummy and easy to suck from a spoon. Then when he's ready, move on to fruit and vegetable purées such as carrot, banana, sweet potato, parsnip, swede, stewed pear or apple, melon and mango. Avoid nuts, salt, honey, high-fibre and low-fat food, tea and coffee and raw or undercooked eggs.

As he gets used to solids you can gradually start introducing more texture and a wider variety of foods. Between seven and nine months he'll probably be on three regular meals a day, trying to feed himself as he gradually gets better at using his hands and fingers, and probably eating the same meals as you – but mashed up. By 12 months, he should be eating a balanced diet including all five food groups: fruit and vegetables, cereals and potatoes, dairy, meat and fish.

But weaning your baby isn't just about getting him used to eating solid foods. If you want your child to share the same healthy and wide-ranging foods as you and escape the junk-food treadmill that so many children today get stuck on, now's the time to think about how and what you give him to eat.

Helping him enjoy mealtimes, and offering him a wide range of fresh, wholesome food will encourage him to develop healthy eating habits that will not only do him good now, but into the future too.

● Get your baby used to eating fresh, unprocessed food from day one. Packets and jars are useful in an emergency but home-prepared meals made from good-quality raw materials have more natural goodness and won't contain additives which have no nutritional benefit.

● When you don't have the time or the means to cook, choose an organic brand of ready-prepared baby food if you can as these tend to be more like home-made food.

● Only offer one new food every two or three days so that if there's any sign of an allergic reaction (tummy ache, diarrhoea, rashes) you can easily identify the culprit. If there is a family history of wheat or dairy allergies avoid giving these foods before 12 months.

● Offer him cooled, boiled tap water (or freshly opened mineral – not spring – water) when he's thirsty. You will find it much harder to wean him on to water when he's older if he has already developed a taste for sweet sugary drinks.

- Make mealtimes fun. Although at times it will feel like a chore, the more you appear to enjoy feeding him the happier your baby will be to eat. Chat to him while preparing his meal, give him lots of praise and encouragement and, once he can sit up in a highchair, try to eat together as a family as often as you can.

- Encourage him to try a wide range of food as this gives him the best chance of having a healthy, balanced diet. If he doesn't accept a new food straightaway don't worry. It's normal to have to offer a new taste 10 to 20 times before it's accepted, so try again another day.

- Understand your child's needs in order to help create happy mealtimes. Tiredness, for example, will mean a loss of appetite; slow eaters need plenty of time; fussy eaters respond best to being given a choice.

> *'I love food – and I hope, as she gets older, Josie will too! Right now I'm introducing her to all my favourite vegetables – puréed broccoli and sweet potato are getting the thumbs up but she spat the swede right out. Never mind. I'll try her with it again next week.'*
>
> Stacey, mum to Josie, aged six and a half months

Helping your baby sleep through the night

For most new parents a night of unbroken sleep is the holy grail. You adore your baby but having to leave your bed in the middle of the night to give him a cuddle or a feed is pure torture, and you long for the night when he'll sleep through without a peep.

The quest for a good night's sleep isn't purely selfish. Sleep is vital for your baby too. During the early weeks and months, for example, his brain is incredibly active: growing, making new connections, taking in new information. When he sleeps, this information is processed and stored for future reference. Sleep helps him to develop physically too. It's during sleep, for example, that growth hormones are released, and new cells grow fastest.

As he gets older, lack of sleep could affect his appetite, weaken his immune system and increase the risk of catching viruses and infections.

While he's tiny, because he's growing at such an amazing rate, he needs to wake frequently to refuel. So, although he may be sleeping for as many as 18 hours out of 24, he'll take his sleep in relatively short stretches, leaving you feeling shattered. Very occasionally some newborn babies will give their lucky parents an unbroken night's sleep after six or eight weeks. But most (especially breastfed) babies won't manage more than five hours or so at a stretch until they are at least three months old.

As he gets older, however (and usually by around six months), your baby will be able to feed enough during his waking hours to sustain him for longer stretches during the night. Sleep will then also become more important for his well-being. By six months or so, for example, he'll need only 12–14 hours of sleep in a 24-hour period, including a couple of one- or two-hour naps. And not enough could make your otherwise happy baby difficult and maybe less responsive.

But even when your baby can physically manage to sleep through the night, there's no guarantee that he will. He may still wake and demand a feed out of habit or comfort. He may be ill, teething or experiencing separation anxiety (see Chapter 8, page 64). Or he may wake because of his sleep pattern – like adults, babies alternate between light and deep sleep. If he wakes during a period of light sleep and opens his eyes, he'll probably cry if he can't see or feel you.

No parent can survive indefinitely on broken nights without it impacting on their relationship, work and health. And the older your baby gets, the more difficult it will become to break the pattern. So while you might adore watching your tiny baby drift off in your arms every night, imagine how you might feel in five months' time when he refuses to sleep anywhere but with you; and dinner, your night out, a relaxing bath or time with your partner has to be cancelled.

For your baby, finding out how to fall asleep without props is something he can only discover with your help. And developing the habit now, like learning how to enjoy good food, will help keep him happy and healthy as he gets older.

Helping your baby fall asleep

- Recognise that your baby needs to learn how to fall asleep on his own. If he is always allowed to drop off while being rocked, cuddled, sung to or fed, when he does wake in the night he'll panic, cry out and only settle with your help.

- Start by establishing a bedtime routine as soon as you can. Most sleep experts agree that this helps babies to recognise the cues that tell them it's time to sleep. And it's never too early, or too late, to start. A typical routine would be bath, feed, cuddle, into the cot, a kiss goodnight then lights out – all taking no more than about 45 minutes.

- Make sure he's awake (with eyes open) when you put him into his cot. It's important that he learns to recognise this cue for falling asleep. If he's allowed to fall asleep in your arms, his pushchair, car seat or bouncy chair, when he wakes up he may feel panicky and cry out.

- Use a similar routine for daytime naps. Make sure the room is dark and quiet, put him into his cot while he's relaxed and calm, and leave him to settle himself.

- Expect him to cry for a little while, at least in the beginning, and try not to go back to him straightaway. If you are concerned, peep in and check that he's safe. He probably just needs a chance to cry, settle and then wait for sleep.

> *'A friend of mine had a year of bad nights with her little one. I know I can't cope without enough sleep so I was determined that Fred would love his cot. I've always put him to sleep there, and it seems to work. When it's nap time, he might whimper for a few minutes but more often he fiddles with his toys, squirms around, then drops off.'*
>
> Sally, mum to Fred, aged seven months

- If he does wake up in the night, stay calm. Picking him up and cuddling him back to sleep may be the fastest option, but it will also confuse him and prolong (rather than prevent) night-time waking. Use the same technique as before. See that he's safe, kiss him good night and leave the room. Your baby knows you love him, and while initially it might be emotionally draining, it will be worth persevering.

Keeping up to date with health checks and immunisations

You are not alone in wanting to ensure that your baby stays fit and well. During his first year he'll have at least four main health checks with your GP or health visitor, including a developmental review when he is between six and nine months old. Attending these checks and reviews is vital for making sure your baby is developing as expected. If there are any problems – for example, with his hearing, or growth rate – the earlier these are spotted, the better chance your baby has of being successfully treated.

In his first year your baby will also be offered a range of immunisations to protect against major childhood diseases, including diptheria, whooping cough, tetanus, Hib (haemophilus influenza type b), meningitis C, pneumococcus and polio. At around 12 months babies are also offered their first MMR (measles, mumps and rubella) vaccination.

Given recent public debate over the safety of MMR, you may find yourself uncertain as to whether or not your baby should have the vaccine. A study carried out in 1996 suggested there may be a link between the MMR vaccine and the medical conditions autism and inflammatory bowel disease. Since then, however, this issue has been looked at by doctors in many different countries as well as the WHO (World Health Organisation). The conclusion appears to be that there is no evidence that the MMR vaccine causes either autism or bowel disorders.

Some parents have tried to avoid the decision by having their children vaccinated separately. But there's no evidence that doing this reduces any of the risks, assuming they exist. Also, during the time lapse between each vaccine, the child is left vulnerable to infection. Once immunity in the general population starts to fall, it's inevitable there will be an outbreak. In fact, there have already been small outbreaks of mumps and measles. And children who haven't or can't (for medical reasons) be immunised, as well as very young babies, are then put at risk of catching these diseases, which can cause serious and occasionally life-threatening complications.

Of course, the final decision whether or not to immunise lies with you, and while so far there is no evidence to suggest that the MMR vaccine is anything other than safe and effective, peace of mind is important, especially where your child is concerned. So if you have any worries, talk to your GP or health visitor. As with many health issues, the better informed you are, the easier you'll find it to make the right decision.

Ensuring a safe, healthy environment

Keeping your baby healthy and safe also means taking a fresh look at your lifestyle – and your baby's lifestyle.

- Give your baby a chance to exercise. He can't move if he's strapped up all day in his buggy, car seat or highchair. Let him lie on a warm rug so he can work his arms and legs; once he's crawling give him lots of space to move around. Even at this age exercise is vital for strengthening his muscles, for improving his balance and control and for developing his heart, lungs and limbs.

- Keep the house smoke-free. Babies are especially vulnerable to the effects of passive smoking. Breathing tobacco smoke makes them prone to chronic coughs and bronchitis, and increases the risk of cot death. If you or your partner is finding it hard to stop smoking, ask your doctor to refer you to a support group (see Further Sources of Information, page 153).

- Get plenty of fresh air. Take your baby out in the pushchair every day, even if he's fast asleep. A dose of sunlight will help stimulate the production of vitamin D, which is vital for healthy bone development.

- Cover your baby up in the sun. A baby's skin is much thinner than an adult's and more prone to sunburn. On sunny days keep him completely in the shade.

- Be safety conscious. This means always thinking ahead to the next stage of your child's development. Babies under one, for example, are most often hurt through falls, so never leave your baby unattended on any raised surface from which he might wriggle or roll. Once your little one is crawling, fit safety gates on the stairs and catches on windows. Keep small objects out of reach to avoid choking accidents and never leave your baby alone in the bath – even if it's shallow.

SUMMARY OF CHAPTER 7

Keeping your baby healthy is a big responsibility, but even though some trips to the doctor are inevitable, there's plenty you can do to protect him against illness and accidents.

- Breastfeed for as along as you can, don't wean him too early and think about how and what you give him to eat. Good eating habits established now will last him a lifetime.
- A proper night's sleep is good for your baby's appetite and immune system. Establish a bedtime routine and teach him how to fall asleep without props.
- Make sure your baby is up to date with his health checks and immunisations.
- Check out your lifestyle and child-proof your house.

CHAPTER 8

Your Happy Baby

Your first year with your baby will be packed with memorable moments, but the most special will be those when your baby seemed happiest – shrieking with delight when you swing her in the play park; waving madly for the camera; devouring her first ice cream. When she's happy, you're happy too. And next to her health, caring for her emotional well-being, her happiness, is one of your main concerns.

Of course, babies cry a lot, especially in the early months. And it would be wrong to assume that because they are crying they are sad. Babies cry because it's the only way they have of communicating. It's a vital part of their survival mechanism, a signal, almost impossible to ignore, that something is wrong.

Given time, you learn how to figure out what each cry means (perhaps hunger, discomfort, over-stimulation) and respond to her needs so she stops crying and starts smiling again.

As your baby gets older, she naturally starts to cry less. From around three months she's starting to notice the world around her so there's more to see and do. She's quickly developing lots of new skills (holding toys, rolling over, babbling), which keep her busy. She's becoming more sociable and enjoys interacting with other people. And you have discovered lots of ways of soothing her when she's unhappy.

Finding out how to keep your baby happy is to some extent a learning curve that's affected by her developing personality and the emotional and physical stages in her development. But being in tune with your baby will help her to feel safe and secure, and build her confidence and self-esteem.

Helping your baby feel special

Ask your antenatal friends round for coffee and chances are you'll not only be comparing how many hours' kip you managed the night before, but also how 'little Arthur is on the go night and day, just like his father' and how 'dear Emily has inherited the family's smiley gene'.

Even at this young age, in a room full of babies it is possible to spot a wide variety of temperaments. Some may be cheerful and adaptable, others irritable and demanding; some will love to be cuddled, and others will only want a hug when it suits them; and some will be outgoing and daring while others might be shy and wary.

Being able to spot traits in your baby will help you to understand her behaviour and needs. For example, having a big first-year birthday bash may not be a good idea if your baby is shy and reserved. If she's very placid and undemanding, you may have to take extra care to give her some one-to-one attention.

Of course, your baby probably has, like most babies, a mixture of all these traits. And while you may find some characteristics more attractive than others, it's important to remember that your baby's personality is still forming and will continue to do so over many months and years. And what form this personality takes will depend to a certain extent on the traits she has inherited as well as her daily experiences and interactions with you and others close to her.

Whatever your baby's emerging personality, try to nurture her as an individual. Helping your child to develop a strong sense of self will give her a firm emotional foundation from which to grow.

- Help your baby feel special. Give her lots of hugs, kisses and smiles. Your love will help her feel valued.

- Praise all your baby's achievements, even if it's just waving at you or banging two bricks together. Your encouragement will boost her self-esteem.

- Tune into your baby's needs. Noticing when she's scared, excited or bored will help her to feel important and loved.

- Nurture the positive aspects of your baby's character. Tell her how cheerful, friendly, caring or brave she is – to bring out the best in her.

- If she is shy, demanding or fussy, remember to be supportive. Give her the extra time, patience and attention she needs now, and remind yourself that she won't always be like this.

- Be aware of promoting gender differences. Often parents are gentle with girls, and more physical with boys. By encouraging your boy's nurturing side or stimulating your little girl's sense of independence, you can avoid sexual stereotyping and allow your baby to develop as an individual.

- Let your baby do things for herself. Every little achievement, from reaching out to grab her favourite soft toy, to holding her own beaker, will increase her sense of self.

'Compared to other babies, Fergus always seemed miserable. He cried at loud noises, didn't enjoy his food, and slept badly. Now he's crawling he seems so much happier – perhaps he just has a strong streak of independence.'

Sally, mum to Fergus, aged ten months

Helping your baby feel secure

For the first few months of her life your baby may be more than happy to be passed around relatives and friends like a box of chocolates. And it's so satisfying to bask in the compliments – 'she's so easy-going, so sociable'. Any time between seven and nine months, however, you may notice a change. Increasingly she starts to stick to you like toffee. She howls if you leave the room without her, glares at anyone she doesn't see at least every day, and clings to you like a baby koala whenever you take her somewhere new.

It's normal for babies at this age to start developing fears – fear of strangers, strange places and strange sounds. More than anything she fears being left without you. For the first six months or so of her life, she imagined that you were simply an extension of herself. Now, slowly, as she starts to develop a sense of herself as an individual, she simultaneously realises that you are a separate person. And this thought makes her anxious and worried about losing you. She's become so attached to you that she's inconsolable if you leave her alone – even for a minute. She doesn't understand yet that you will return.

While some experience it more intensely than others, all babies go through separation and stranger anxiety. It's a major emotional milestone, often starting at around seven months and for some children continuing until they are two years or older. Unfortunately, the inevitable onset of separation and stranger anxiety often coincides with the parent's return to work. But while it's upsetting, and sometimes frustrating, to deal with, your baby's desire to be with you is a good sign: it shows that she's developing a strong attachment to you.

Helping your baby deal with this stage in her life will not only make it less traumatic for you and her, but also strengthen the bond between you. And while personality will play a role, generally speaking, the more secure your baby feels, the faster and more smoothly she'll pass through this stage. A secure child feels confident enough to leave the ones she loves, and for them to leave her.

- Make sure your baby knows that you love and care for her. Be consistent and respond to her cries, smiles or other signals with sensitivity and confidence.

- Always reassure your baby that you're coming back. If you need to leave her to go into another room, tell her where you are going and that you'll be back in a minute. If she cries, call out that you're on your way back. Gradually she'll learn that you mean what you say.

- Let your baby set the pace. Don't force her to be friendly. Even relatives who she hasn't seen for a few days may upset her without intending to. Remind family members and friends that a softly-softly approach is needed.

- Act calmly. When you need to leave her, give her a hug and a kiss and go without a fuss. If you look calm and happy she'll be reassured.

- Let your baby have some independence. Allowing her to crawl into another room, for example, will help build her confidence about new places.

- Allow your baby to have a comforter. Many babies become naturally attached to a special object, like a blanket or a soft toy, which they insist on taking everywhere with them. These can be especially reassuring for babies at this stage in their lives when they need something to hold on to that represents security.

- Get your baby used to socialising. Mother and toddler groups are ideal for building your baby's confidence. She can explore new places and new toys, and meet new people, knowing all the time that you are there, within sight, if she needs you.

> *'Joe went through a very timid patch. I remember from about eight months how he'd bury his head in my shoulder whenever we went into the local shop – even though we'd been going since he was born. He's not like that now; in fact, if I let him, he'd be quite happy to go into the shop on his own.'*
>
> Caroline, mum to Joe, aged two and a half

Keeping your baby stimulated

When you think about how your baby started life – as a tiny bundle with barely any sense of the world around her – you can only be amazed by her mastery of physical and mental skills over the coming months and years.

In her first year, especially, she'll reach many important milestones. She'll learn, for example, how to sit, crawl, pull herself up to standing, cruise while holding on to furniture and maybe even walk a few steps on her own. She'll be able to feed herself finger food, point with a finger and pick up tiny objects with her forefinger and thumb. She'll understand the meaning of 'no' and enjoy imitating people. She'll babble, respond to simple commands, recognise her own name and try to imitate words. And she'll be able to solve simple problems (find hidden objects easily, for example), understand cause and effect (when she shakes the rattle it makes a noise) and start to understand how objects are used (drink from a cup, brush her hair, listen into a telephone).

Your baby's natural way of learning is through play and exploration. For example, when she crawls over a mountain of cushions, she's discovering how to balance and coordinate her limbs. When you sing her favourite nursery rhyme again and again, she's starting to understand the basis of language. And playing peek-a-boo teaches her about object permanence – just because she can't see it, doesn't mean it's not there.

How is she motivated? Partly it's an instinctive drive to discover and learn, but also it's down to your encouragement and support. When, for example, she manages her first wave goodbye, your praise and enthusiasm for her achievement boosts her self-esteem and convinces her that learning is fun.

Encouraging your baby to reach her natural milestones also enables her to start interacting with the wider world. Once she can sit up, for example, everything around her looks different. Once she can hold on to something, she can put it in her mouth – a favourite way to explore and discover. (Do take care that she can't get her hands on anything that could harm her – see Chapter 7, page 61.) When she can move, she can reach that toy that looks so interesting. When you pull a funny face, she can pull one back.

There's a fine balance, however, between stretching a child and pushing her too hard. Your aim isn't to have the first baby on the block who can walk or clap or spell her own name, but to build your baby's confidence so that when she's ready to try a new skill, she believes she can succeed. The more confident she feels when she tries, the better chance she has of success, and the happier she'll feel about herself.

It's also important to remember that every child develops differently, and the time it takes to reach each milestone will vary from baby to baby. Also, when babies are ready to develop a new skill (like walking), other skills (like language development) are often put on hold for a while.

Whatever the rate of your baby's progress, much of her motivation and success will depend on the kind of stimulation and attention she receives from you.

- Play with your baby. Not only does this bring you closer together, but your interaction will also help her to develop important social skills like learning how to take turns and share. Look at books together; fill a basin and splash, pour and fill cups and jugs; chase her on all fours around the sitting room and make an obstacle course out of cushions for her to manoeuvre over and around.

- Include your baby. Even everyday chores are fun when you're doing them for the first time. Let her help with dusting the television or combing her hair.

- Give her lots of praise whenever you have the chance.

- Encourage independence. Don't be tempted to jump in too quickly and help when she's attempting something new. If she can find out how to put the shapes into the sorter by herself or slip her own arm into her coat, this gives you a chance to praise her and boost her sense of achievement.

- Allow her safe areas to explore. Your baby is naturally curious and can find out lots about the world on her own, while developing her sense of adventure. Kitchen cupboards are especially fun, so why not allocate one just for her, and fill it with safe items such as saucepans, wooden spoons, plastic bowls, etc?

- Talk to her as much as you can. Chatting while you're getting on with chores will not only help her to feel involved but will also help to develop her social and language skills. Once she starts babbling, remember to pause to give her a chance to 'chatter' back.

- Give her time to play on her own when she's in the mood. Keep an interesting selection of toys and activities to hand and choose a good moment (perhaps when she's fresh from a nap but not hungry) to encourage her to play on her own. But don't expect too much – at this age her concentration span is still very short.

'Mimi was desperate to crawl. She was so frustrated just sitting and not being able to move. Once she was able to support herself on her hands and knees, I'd roll a soft ball towards her. She'd become really excited and stretch out to try to reach it. Eventually she was able to wiggle forward and grab it. She was clearly delighted but also exhausted!'

Simone, mum to Mimi, aged one

SUMMARY OF CHAPTER 8

- Making sure your baby feels special will help her to develop a strong sense of self.
- Stranger and separation anxiety are natural milestones. Helping her feel secure will help her move faster and more smoothly through these stages.
- Keeping your baby stimulated and giving her lots of encouragement and support will build her confidence.

CHAPTER 9

Going Back to Work

M ore mothers now work than ever before, but that doesn't mean that the decision – to work or not to work – is always an easy one.

Of course, for some mothers there is no dilemma. Perhaps you have always known that when you have children you want to be at home with them full time, and can't wait to give up work. Or perhaps you have to go back to work because financially it's a case of sink or swim. If you are bringing up your child on your own, or your partner is on a low income, an extra salary can make all the difference between just getting by and being financially free to enjoy the extras, like holidays and outings.

For some mums, however, there is no right or wrong answer. You may, for example, love your job, want to keep up your skills and worry that being at home all day will drive you mad. At the same time you want to do what's best for your child, and when you look at it from a child's point of view, having mummy at home is the obvious choice.

For lots of mums struggling with this problem, flexible working (part time or based at home) can be a solution, although it's worth bearing in mind that even these scenarios aren't always ideal. Part-timers, for example, often feel they are cramming a full-time job into half the time for half the pay. And working from home can leave you feeling isolated and out of the loop.

Ultimately, you need to make a choice that's right for you all as a family. If you do go back to work, full or part time, it's helpful to know that there's no evidence to show that if children of working parents are well loved and well cared for, they are any less likely to thrive than if one parent stays at home. And if you enjoy your work and have good childcare, your child can reap a number of benefits – a great role model for a mum, a family that pulls together to make it work, plus more loving, attentive people in his life.

Getting a happy balance between work and family life can, however, be challenging. Even if you love your job and have found a great nanny, childminder or nursery, you may struggle with feelings of guilt. Finding, and keeping, good childcare takes time, energy and lots of emotional input. And leaving your child with someone else, even if he is settled and happy, can be hard.

Knowing what to look for will help you to find the right person to care for your baby, and getting prepared (both on a practical and emotional level) will help make the transition between being at home and returning to work easier for you both.

Finding the right childcare

The most difficult, but also the most crucial, part of finding good childcare is judging the character and abilities of the caregiver, especially as you may only have the opportunity to meet him or her a few times before handing over your baby. The only way you can feel happy about the caregiver's abilities and dedication is by checking references and watching her at work for a day or two.

So what are your choices? If you have a close relative living nearby who is willing to care for your baby, this can be the perfect option. Otherwise, there are various alternatives, depending on your finances and personal preferences.

For example, there are many advantages to having your baby cared for in your own home by a nanny or au pair. Your baby will be in a familiar environment, getting individual attention, and your life will be made easier as you won't have to transport him each morning and night. But although nannies are expensive (though sharing one can bring down the cost), they don't have to be registered, so the onus on checking her references and suitability lies with you; and if she's alone with your baby it will be difficult to check that she's doing a good job. Au pairs cost less but they usually live in, and as they have no qualifications in childcare should not be given sole responsibility for a baby.

Another option is a day nursery. These have to be registered with the local authority so can offer a certain amount of reassurance about the quality of care. You can also speak to other parents who take their child there. As there will be a number of staff, you won't be affected if one of them is unwell. And for toddlers and pre-schoolers especially, being raised with other children will offer lots of fun and a chance to develop good social skills. On the down side, day nurseries can be very expensive (especially if you have more than one child), the hours will be less flexible than with a home carer, and your child will always be competing for attention with other children.

Childminders (women who care for children in their own home) are often the most affordable type of childcare. By law they must be registered with their local authority and there is a strict child–adult ratio. Your child will be in a family environment, joining in with household activities and there may be other children to play with. And if you have any concerns, you can talk to other parents who use the same childminder.

Finding the right childcare takes time and research so it makes sense to look into the options available to you sooner rather than later. If you are thinking about a day nursery, for example, visit several, then go back and spend some time in your favourites to see how the staff relate to the children. Talk to other parents with children at the nursery and find out what they like and dislike about it. If you're visiting a childminder, there will be specific questions you'll want to ask: Does she have a first-aid qualification? What kind of food does she cook? What activities does she enjoy doing with the children? Always ask for and carefully check references. You may feel embarrassed about appearing intrusive, but where your child's safety is concerned you'll want to be as careful as possible.

Lots of mums have an instinct for who they feel would be the right person to look after their baby. But while choosing someone who shares your views on how to look after children and who you can get on with is important, it's the relationship she'll have with your baby that really counts. The best way of making a choice is to watch your potential carer in action with other babies or children so you see just how child-friendly she really is. For example:

- Is she warm and responsive? Babies need lots of cuddles and understanding.

- Does she watch and listen carefully? The more in tune she is with your baby, the better she'll be able to understand and respond to his needs.

- Is she playful and imaginative? As your baby gets older, he'll benefit from more stimulation, and love playing games and being creative.

- Can she chat easily to little ones? Talking to your baby helps him feel special, and will encourage him to start communicating too.

- Is she patient? Your baby needs to be able to go at his own pace, whether he's being fed, comforted or played with.

- Can she join in without taking over? Your baby can only learn if he's given the chance.

- Can she spot difficult situations before they arise? Noticing that your baby is ready for bed before he becomes overtired, for example, will help prevent tears and upset.

'We've found a wonderful childminder who lives close by. She has young children herself, which I think makes her more sympathetic to Erin's needs.'

Anne, mum to Erin, aged 18 months

Preparing for the change

When you've had many months at home, safe and snug in your new world with your new baby, the thought of venturing back to work and leaving your child with another person may, at times, seem unbearable – and something you'd rather not think about. But while your maternity leave is precious, it makes sense to use the time to think ahead about the challenges you'll face when you return to work, as getting prepared now will help to reduce the inevitable practical and emotional stresses.

Once you've found a carer you like and trust, your greatest

concern will be that your baby settles quickly and is happy. And there's plenty you can do to smooth the way.

● Most importantly you need to get your baby to start drinking from a bottle at least two weeks (if not more) before your start date. If you are breastfeeding you don't need to give up, as you can either express enough to cover his needs during the day or give him formula during the day and breastfeed him before you leave for work and when you get home.

● In the last few weeks before your start date, make a note of your baby's routine (when he feeds, when he has a nap, etc) so that your carer can keep to the same pattern. The less disruption your baby has to cope with, the faster he'll settle.

● Try to spend as much time as possible together – you, your baby and his new carer. Babies need time to warm to strangers, and a good carer will be aware of this. At the first meeting, keep your baby on your lap to start with, then, when he seems relaxed, encourage your carer to make eye contact and talk to him. If he's comfortable with the conversation, put your baby on the floor with a favourite toy and invite your carer to come closer and play with the toy. Going at your baby's pace will help him to accept someone new in his life more readily.

> *'Getting Lauren to take a bottle was a real struggle. She's always been breastfed, and just didn't seem to like the feel of a synthetic teat. My start date back at work was looming but how could I contemplate leaving her at the nursery if she wouldn't feed from a bottle? Finally I had to leave her with my husband for the day. She held out as long as she could then I think hunger got the better of her.'*
>
> Sophie, mum to Lauren, aged six months

Making it work

When the day comes for you to say goodbye and set off for work, you need to be prepared for some upset. If your baby is going through separation anxiety, for example (see Chapter 8, page 64), he's likely to be more clingy than usual and have no idea when, or even if, you are going to return. Trying to keep the situation happy and calm, even if you feel in complete turmoil, will reassure him. Prepare him in advance. Tell him that you'll be leaving in 10 or 15 minutes, so that your departure doesn't come as a shock. And avoid long goodbyes. Kiss him goodbye, give him a hug and then go without any fuss.

You may find that your baby settles quickly and is soon happily waving you goodbye through the sitting room or nursery window. Some babies, however, always fret when they are left, in which case you may want to peep back through the window after a few minutes to be reassured that he's fine.

On your return, try to be matter of fact and calm again. You may feel very emotional, but your baby will be unsettled by any unusual strength of feeling, and is likely to burst into tears himself. He may, however, naturally cry – double-checking that you still love him by asking for lots of attention is quite normal, even when he's been perfectly happy all day without you.

Meanwhile, building a good relationship and treating your baby's carer as a partner will help motivate her to keep up good standards of care. For example, helping to tidy up at the end of the day, chatting about what's happened, and saying thank you for the day's work will always be appreciated. And talking about problems sooner rather than later will prevent issues growing out of perspective.

The first few weeks back at work will leave you exhausted. You now have another important person in your life to consider, as well as less time to manage your home and find time for yourself and your partner. For your baby, no amount of extra household income will substitute for a relaxed and happy home environment, free of stress and conflict. So it's important that you and your partner are supportive of each other. Sharing the childcare responsibilities (see Chapter 6, page 48) and household chores, for example, will help to prevent resentment building up.

'When I went back to work I really fretted about missing some of Josh's major milestones – like his first step, or his first word. But I know that's more about me and my needs than his. I try to remind myself that his welfare is more important – being loved, and well cared for.'

Valerie, mum to Josh, aged nine months

SUMMARY OF CHAPTER 9

- If a child is well loved and well cared for there is no evidence to show that he won't continue to thrive if you go back to work, and having the chance to develop other warm and loving relationships is good for your baby.
- Finding good childcare takes time so start looking sooner rather than later.
- Make sure you see potential carers in action with other babies and children to see how child-friendly they are.
- Prepare for the change. Get your baby used to drinking from a bottle at least two weeks before your start date back at work, make a note of your baby's typical day for his carer and try to allow for your baby to spend as much time as possible with his new carer before you leave them together.
- Always let your baby know that you'll be leaving shortly. Avoid long goodbyes and emotional reunions – but be prepared for tears!
- Build a good relationship with your baby's carer.
- Work at maintaining harmony in the home.

CHAPTER 10

Your Healthy, Happy Pre-schooler

Your growing toddler has a natural drive towards independence, and although there will be times when it's quicker and easier for you to wash her face, pour her drink or fetch her coat, now's the time to start encouraging her to do things for herself.

But don't expect too much maturity too soon. Although she's desperate to be in charge, she will still often feel anxious about the world around her, and it will be many years before she can really make sense of it. So one minute she'll be clinging to you, the next running in the opposite direction; she's relying on you to make her feel safe and secure, yet at the same time she wants to take control.

Lots of the issues that you face over the following few months will stem from her need to exert her will. How you respond will have a big impact on the way she learns to cope and her feelings about herself. Tuning into her needs, encouraging her and praising her achievements, and consistently offering her warmth and security will help her to feel happy, capable and special.

And you'll soon reap the rewards. Between the ages of three and four, as she leaps from toddlerhood into childhood you'll notice that she's altogether easier than she was a year or so ago. By managing and encouraging her growing sense of independence, you will enable her to develop the sense of self-control she needs to help manage her emotions. And your continuing love, warmth and praise will help her to develop a strong sense of self-esteem that will stay with her as she goes on to school and beyond.

Managing mealtimes

From around 18 months, when your toddler first develops a surge of independence, food inevitably becomes a battleground. Most behaviour, from rejecting food and fussy eating to making a mess and refusing to sit at the table, is perfectly normal. But even so, you may worry about her diet, especially if she decides there is only a handful of foods she's prepared to try.

Trying to understand your toddler's needs may help. At this age, it's natural, for example, to develop strong likes and dislikes. She's becoming her own person, and letting you know about it! Life is exciting, and she may be easily distracted and need help to keep her focused on her food – eating with her at mealtimes will help. Perhaps she's better in the mornings than at lunchtimes, in which case concentrate on breakfasts or an early lunch rather than an evening meal. Perhaps she's naturally slow and needs plenty of time to finish a meal, or is naturally timid and approaches new foods cautiously.

Creating a happy atmosphere around the table is the best way to help your toddler enjoy mealtimes. But don't expect an easy ride as there will always be occasions when she screws up her nose in disgust and tries to get down from the table without even tasting what you've lovingly prepared for her. Try to stay unfazed. Your toddler wants a reaction – to prove that she's in charge – and the less wound up you appear, the faster she'll realise her behaviour is getting her nowhere.

If you're concerned that she is not getting the nutrients she needs, take a long-term view. Instead of considering just what she eats each day, look at what she has over a week. The chances are that once you take breakfasts and snacks into account you'll find she's packing away a more well-balanced diet than you had realised.

Meanwhile, keep focused on what she's eating. The more bad habits she develops now, the harder they will be to break as she gets older.

- Don't start to rely on high-sugar, high-fat food just because it's all she will eat. Once she gets a taste for highly processed foods it will be hard to wean her off them.

- Don't give up just because she rejects a certain food once. It can take 10 to 20 times for a child to see, smell, touch and taste a new food before accepting it.

- Offer her regular, healthy snacks. Small children have high-energy needs, and a small, healthy snack (cracker and cheese, chopped fresh raw fruit, mashed banana on toast) mid-morning and mid-afternoon will quickly revitalise her.

- Accept that she won't like everything you give her but keep offering a wide choice, otherwise she'll become hooked on just a few foods.

- Let her exercise some choice, between two types of fruit, for example, so she has a sense of control.

Having physical fun

As once again you chase after your toddler in the park, you'll be reminded just what an enormous amount of energy children have at this age. Sometimes they can stay on the go until they literally drop – awake and charging about one moment, crashed out and fast asleep in your arms the next.

Keeping up with your child at this age can be exhausting. Once she's been walking for several months she'll discover how to run, jump, kick and throw. And then she'll be putting her new skills to good effect, clambering over sofas, bouncing on the beds and sliding down the stairs.

Finding constructive ways to help your child to let off steam outdoors is good for her health – and for your furniture. Lots of fresh air and exercise will help her to sleep well at night. And getting her body moving will help her to develop spatial understanding and thereby improve her balance and coordination skills. Regular exercise also has a positive effect on the way the brain develops, building up the connections between neurones (neural pathways) in the brain. This is why, for example, learning to ride a bike is a skill you never forget.

How quickly, however, your child learns to pedal (or throw, catch, balance, run or climb) will depend largely on her body build and strength. Some children naturally develop faster in these areas than others. Putting her under pressure to do these things before she's ready could put her off even trying. What's important is that she has a chance to have a go and enjoy herself, as well as encouraging her to see physical activity as a normal part of everyday life.

- Bear in mind that toddlers are generally happier with activities in which parents participate too, while a pre-school child may be content with you just watching.

- Try to organise something active and outdoors for at least part of the day, whether it's a trip to the park, a walk to the local shops or just running around with friends in the garden.

- Stock up on equipment for active fun – a bike, skipping rope, balls of various sizes.

- Sign up for a weekly class. Music and movement and mini gymnastics are good for building muscle strength as well as developing a range of skills like climbing and jumping, and encouraging coordination, balance and agility.

- Make it a family event. Try swimming, a bike ride (piggy-back bikes are great for little ones who are still developing their cycling skills) or a walk in the countryside.

- Incorporate calm, quiet activities too. Little children don't know when to stop, and being overactive can lead to being overtired.

Finding time for play

Whether it's dressing up as a wicked witch, dropping pebbles in a pond, building a tower out of bricks or colouring in a picture, your child is doing so much more than just having fun. Playing is how a child learns – about herself and other people and (crucially) how to survive in the world around her.

In fact, playing is as essential as food, sleep, hugs and kisses for the development of a healthy, happy child. And given the opportunity, children love to do it, especially if you are prepared to get down on your hands and knees and play as well. At this age your child still sees you as her preferred playmate and whether you're up for it or not, she will want you to join in with her activities.

Different types of play help to teach your child different things. For example, messy play (digging holes in the garden, building sandcastles, splashing about in the bath) gives her the chance to find out about the physical world. Physical play (see above) helps her to learn how her body works, develop her problem-solving skills ('I can't get up the tree that way, but I can if I do it like this'). Playing with other children (chasing, make believe, doing a jigsaw together) helps her develop social skills, like communication, cooperation and empathy. Looking at books with you and singing nursery rhymes helps her to understand language and to learn how to talk.

For some parents, mucking in with their children comes naturally. For others, the prospect of crawling around on all fours pretending to be a man-eating lion or emptying the kitchen cupboards to play shops isn't very enticing, especially when the chores are piling up. But these are precious times. There will come a day when you will look back nostalgically at when your child enjoyed your company so much.

This isn't to say, however, that your child can't also play alone. On a practical level, it's impossible to entertain your child every minute of the day. And learning how to play alone is an important skill that helps to develop independence and self-reliance. At this age, however, children don't have a very long attention span, so while it's good to encourage her to play on her own, don't expect her to occupy herself for too long. If there are chores you have to finish tell your child you'll be able to join her in ten minutes and set a timer so she can listen for the bell rather than constantly badger you.

Like toys, televisions and computers are now also part of children's entertainment. But lots of parents worry about their children watching too much television or, with older children, spending too long on the computer.

Television and computers are a fact of life, and if used wisely have lots to offer. There are some great educational, stimulating and fun programmes, which can introduce children to new experiences and ideas and broaden their outlook on the world. And learning how to use a computer is essential in today's world.

The way to avoid the television or computer taking over your child's life is to set limits, making sure that she also has enough time to do all the other activities that are important, such as playing with you, playing with friends, playing by herself and enjoying lots of outdoor physical activities. If you need to keep an eye on how long she spends watching the television or playing on the computer, use a kitchen timer to avoid arguments when the time is up.

Props for play

● Choose toys that are right for your child's age. Those that have lasting value (building or construction kits, for example) are especially worth investing in as you can extend them over the years and they will be played with again and again.

● Provide lots of props for imaginary play, especially dressing-up clothes. Children love make believe, and it's good for them too, stimulating the imagination, creativity and problem-solving skills.

● Stock up on activities that your child can do on her own, like painting and colouring. Having easy access to pens, paper and sticky shapes, and a table that's just the right height for her, will give her the freedom to get creative whenever she feels in the mood.

● Collect together a box of odds and ends (buttons, cereal boxes, yoghurt pots, etc) as these will help to keep her occupied on a rainy day. At this age you need to be prepared for mess, so store a pile of old newspapers for covering the floor as well.

● Check out charity and second-hand shops for simple jigsaw puzzles and board games.

Getting a good night's sleep

Lack of sleep will make your child grouchy and difficult. And she also needs her sleep in order to grow. It's during sleep that growth hormone is released and cells multiply fastest. So, how much sleep is enough? By the age of three, your child will need 9 to 12 hours sleep in every 24.

You may find, however, that getting your child to fall asleep, and stay asleep, is a major challenge, especially if she's moved from cot to bed and can now get out on her own. Toddlers like to have their own way, and often it will seem easier to give in to her demands for another story, a drink of milk or a cuddle on the sofa just for the sake of a quiet evening.

But helping your child to learn what's expected of her at bedtime won't just benefit you. The less tired she is during the day, the better she will enjoy everyday life. The good news is that it's never too late to help your child learn good sleep habits, but it may take a lot of persistence on your part.

- The key is to develop a calming bedtime routine – a relaxing bath, a bedtime story, a goodnight kiss and cuddle, then lights out – so your child knows what's expected of her.

- Make sure the room is a comfortable temperature, quiet and dark. If she prefers, just use a very dim nightlight, as too much light can disturb sleep.

- If your child gets out of bed, always take her straight back – no chat, no stories, just a kiss, a cuddle and lights out again. You may have to do this a few times before she finally drops off but she'll quickly understand that you mean business and each subsequent night should get easier.

- When illness or a holiday upsets your child's sleep patterns try to re-establish the old routine as quickly as you can.

- If nightmares are keeping your child awake don't reinforce these anxieties by checking under the bed for monsters or agreeing to leave a light on. Just reassure her that everyone has dreams and they can't hurt and that when she goes back to sleep they will have vanished.

- Night-terrors (an extreme form of nightmare) can be upsetting. Your child will appear to be wide awake with her eyes open and very scared. Don't wake her – she'll settle down on her own – but do make sure that she can't harm herself.

- If bedwetting is a problem, make sure your child uses the toilet before she goes to sleep, protect the mattress with a waterproof cover and, if an accident happens, reassure your child that it's okay.

Coping with tantrums

Your child's huge drive towards independence comes from realising that you and she are separate, that she's her own person, and that she can make choices and act on them if she wishes. Suddenly she really believes that she can do everything herself, and is desperate to conquer the world, or at least pour her own drink, push the buggy and squeeze the toothpaste.

Allowing her to have a go, even though it may at times slow you down or cause a mess, is essential for her healthy emotional development. The sense of achievement will boost her self-esteem and, in the long run, make her happier.

There are practical reasons for encouraging independence too. She may soon be off to nursery school or you may be planning another baby, in which case you won't always be on hand to help her. You may also be thinking about potty training, and a sense of independence will help to prepare her to take this big step forward.

Despite her desire to be 'grown up', your toddler is, however, still very uncertain of the world. She wants to try to do things for herself, but she's still mastering lots of new skills and needs your help. Knowing when to offer support can be a fine art. While you may need to offer help, you must also allow her to feel as if she's done it on her own. Stepping in and taking over – or refusing to let her try – may leave her feeling furious.

Not all toddlers have tantrums, but difficult behaviour is common from around 18 months onwards. Determined to stretch her developing skills to the limit, your toddler may find she just can't manage, or isn't allowed, to do what she wants. This can result in an explosion of emotions – tears, screams, kicking, hitting – leaving both you and your toddler feeling shaken and exhausted.

Once a rage has taken hold you'll find it impossible to reason or argue with your toddler. Instead, check that she's safe (a child who is thrashing about during a tantrum may hurt herself) and try to carry on as normal until the tantrum has run its course. Once she has calmed down, act as if nothing happened. Telling her off is pointless, especially as she will probably have found the episode as upsetting as you. Instead a reassuring cuddle will help her to feel safe and secure again.

But while tantrums are normal, they don't have to be a feature of everyday life. Most children grow out of them by three or four. Meanwhile, here are some strategies to help side-step difficult behaviour.

- Most tantrums are triggered by upsetting or frustrating events – getting dressed in the morning, for example, or leaving the park after a fun afternoon. Try to spot her flashpoints and ward off a tantrum before it takes hold.

- Build in extra time for your toddler to try, for example, dressing herself, rather than saying no because you are in a hurry.

- Whenever you can, give her choices, such as 'Would you like to wear the blue jumper or the red one?', so she has some sense of control.

- Use distraction to avert a tantrum. When you sense your toddler is getting worked up, try offering her a favourite toy, or talk to her calmly and quietly about something completely different.

- Low blood sugar levels can affect a small child's moods so try to avoid long stretches without food. Keeping some healthy snacks on hand can help.

- Make sure she has regular opportunities to let off steam (see Having physical fun, page 79).

SUMMARY OF CHAPTER 10

For toddlers and pre-schoolers, lots of issues stem from a natural need to assert themselves. How you respond will impact on how your child learns to cope and her feelings about herself.

- Mealtimes often become a battleground. Creating a happy atmosphere around the table while continuing to offer a healthy, varied diet will help to lay the foundations for a healthy future.

- Regular physical exercise will help your child to let off steam while building strength and stamina.

- Make sure your child has time to play as this is vital for learning about the world around her, developing independence and self-reliance; and when you play with her, it is a great opportunity to bond.

- It's never too late to establish good sleep habits. Sleep helps your child to grow, and also helps her to manage her emotions.

- Tantrums at this age are normal, but they don't have to be a feature of everyday life. Encourage independence and head off a rage when you can.

CHAPTER 11

Education

In the formal sense, your child's education begins on his first day at school, but he's naturally been learning about the world around him from the moment he was born. And by naturally stimulating and supporting him, you've helped him to develop a real love of learning.

Encouraging a love of learning is one of the best ways you can help your child succeed at school, so how can you keep this up? Bombarding him with facts and figures will be the quickest way to turn him off. Instead the key is to make learning fun (see Finding time for play, page 80), keep it within your child's ability range and make it part of your everyday life. Reading books together, for example, will be a pleasurable activity for both of you, and as language acquisition is one of the most important factors in determining a child's academic success, regular story times will naturally increase your child's comprehension and vocabulary.

Once your child starts at school, the learning process is to a certain extent taken out of your hands. But that doesn't mean it's no longer within your influence. From choosing a school to supporting their learning at home, there's still lots you can do to make sure your child's school life is happy and productive.

'Going to the library has been part of our weekly routine ever since Jason was tiny. My husband and I read a lot – and now Jason loves books too.'

Ros, mum to Jason, aged six

Choosing a school

You want your child to be happy, to learn and do well. This makes choosing a school seem simple, but with Ofsted reports and school league tables to plough through, local gossip and a generally competitive culture to contend with, choosing a school for your child – whatever his age and stage – can cause real emotional turmoil.

Often, even when you've done all the groundwork you could possibly do, it's still hard to really see how effective a school is until your child has been there for a few years. Meanwhile, teachers can move on and heads can change.

Of course, if you want your child to go to a school that's very popular you may find that the school is choosing you rather than vice versa. There will be a pecking order (beginning with catchment) and if your application doesn't fulfil the necessary criteria you may have to accept a place in a school that wouldn't be your first choice.

If this does happen, or the school proves to be the wrong choice, bear in mind that you may be able to move your child at a later date. Although this may not seem ideal, when children are young they are very adaptable.

Whatever the outcome, it is important to appear confident (to your child at least) about the school he is going to, as this will help him get his new life off to a positive and enthusiastic start.

Playgroup/nursery

At this age the most important lessons your child should be learning are about getting along with others, and this should be fun. Make a short list of local playgroups and/or nurseries and try to spend a morning at each one. The emphasis should be on play, and the atmosphere should be caring, happy and positive. Try to imagine your toddler there. Would he respond well to the way the sessions are structured? Would he enjoy the activities on offer? Feeling you could talk a problem over easily with the staff, and that your presence is welcomed, is important too.

First school

Practical considerations are important. Distance from home, for example, will affect how your child travels to school. Being able to walk is a huge bonus. It is good for your child's health, and also his social life as a neighbourhood school means friends are more likely to live close by. The size of the school may also be an issue. You may feel a quieter child will thrive better in a smaller school, whereas a larger school may be able to offer more facilities and opportunities.

Look at the school's Ofsted report (available from the school or on the internet) – this will give you a good insight into the school's ethos, strengths and weaknesses. SATs (Standard Attainment Tests) results are interesting but bear in mind that the social background of the school's intake will also be significant. Talk to other parents but make up your own mind by visiting the school. Are the classrooms stimulating and colourful with plenty of the children's work on the walls? How do the children act during lessons? Some busy noise is inevitable, but can the teacher easily grab their attention? Do they look interested? And find out about sport provision and extra-curricula activities such as music, art, dance and drama.

Secondary school

Start sooner rather than later visiting schools on open days. This will give you a chance to talk to teachers and have a good look around at the facilities. But try to visit during a normal school day too as seeing the school in action will give you a better sense of the atmosphere and the opportunity to talk to pupils for an inside view. Watch the children during class. Are they attentive? Do they seem happy? Are the teachers lively and keen?

Again Ofsted reports and league tables are helpful, but try to focus on your child's needs. Does he thrive in a competitive atmosphere or need more nurturing? Does the school value effort as much as achievement? If your child loves sport or drama or music, does the school offer enough opportunities to keep him interested?

Make sure your child is involved in the process. He should visit with you and express his own views. If going to the same school as his friends is important, try to take this into account. But while having chums on those first few days will help your child to settle in more quickly, every school will have children who don't know anyone else, and your child will quickly make new friends.

> 'Where we live all the popular schools are always oversubscribed. Zanthe didn't get into our first choice, and I think my anxieties made it hard for her to settle initially. I've since tried to be much more positive – and now she seems happier.'
>
> Zoe, mum to Zanthe, aged 11

Supporting your child

Every parent wants his or her child to have a happy and productive school life. And chances are, if your child is happy, he'll do well too. For children, being happy at school depends on having friends (some children are happy with one or two – others like to have a gang of mates), feeling relaxed and respected (a caring and positive environment), and being stimulated by the work and supported by their teachers and parents.

Supporting your child, however, may not always be easy. Just finding out what's happened during the day can be a struggle if your child is particularly reticent, but at least while your child is at primary school you can meet up with other parents at the school gate and pick up snippets about what's happening. Once your child goes to secondary school, however, you're more likely to feel out of the loop. There are fewer natural opportunities to meet other parents, chat to teachers and generally keep in touch.

Homework can also be an issue. Few children actively enjoy doing it – so how can you encourage them to settle down and get it out of the way without it turning into a daily battle? And while it's important to show your child that you value education, how do you do this without piling on the pressure but at the same time encouraging them to become independent learners?

Keeping track

- Get involved in school life. Joining the PTA, offering support at events, helping on school trips, making friends with other parents are all ways in which you can keep track of what's going on.

- Encourage school talk. Bear in mind that like lots of adults, children don't always want to discuss the day's work when they get home, but a few open-ended questions – Did you have a hot or cold lunch today? What did the art teacher think of your homework? Who did you sit next to in assembly? – will help to elicit more than a yes or no answer.

- Invite your child's friends round for tea. Invariably children end up talking about school when they are all together and you'll be able to pick up lots of interesting snippets while preparing their food.

'It's much easier to stay in touch if your child goes to a local secondary school. You're more likely to know other mums with children at the same school, and they can help fill in the gaps!'

Annabel, mum to Eleanor, aged 13

Encouraging good homework habits

Your child is likely to have homework even from an early age. By helping him to get into good habits from the start, you will be supporting his education and helping him to achieve his potential.

- Establish with your child a set time for homework, for example after tea but before watching television or using the computer.

- Create a quiet and comfortable space for doing homework. Older children may happily go off to their room, but younger children especially may not like being closeted away on their own and you may need to make space on the kitchen table.

- Encourage your child to do his homework on his own. If he needs help, give him advice but don't do the homework for him. If he still can't manage, write a note to his teacher so your child can get the extra support he needs.

- Support your child by getting clued up and pointing him in the right direction for help and information. Ask the school for advice on revision aids, for example, or take advantage of the many websites that contain education pages which follow the national curriculum.

- Help keep distractions to a minimum – radio, television, younger siblings.

- Reward him when he's put in lots of effort – a few words of praise, a cup of hot chocolate or fruit juice when he finishes, extra time watching television or on the computer.

- At secondary school especially, when homework demands increase significantly, encourage him to be organised – an in tray and an out tray, for example, a prominent timetable for easy checking.

Valuing your child

Your reaction to what your child does at school is important.

- Remember that school life isn't just about getting great grades. Making good friends, discovering new interests and just being willing to take part are equally important, and should be applauded as much as subject success.

- Reward your child for his efforts as much as his achievements. Trying hard, especially in areas that don't come naturally to your child, deserves just as much praise.

- Be supportive but avoid putting on pressure. Your child is then more likely to take responsibility for his own work, and more likely to value his work for itself rather than because it pleases you.

- Show an interest. Reading your child's set text for English, visiting an historic attraction relevant to his history work, even having a go at some of his sums will show him you value the work he's doing but also create a point of contact.

Handling problems

When you child faces a problem at school, either with friends or teachers, your natural instinct is to charge in and get it sorted. The protective urge can be overwhelming, but sometimes – especially as your child gets older – it's of more value to offer support and advice from the sidelines rather than jumping in and possibly adding to the problem.

Teachers

- Concerned about your child's development? Parents' evenings offer a formal opportunity to talk with teachers. Go prepared with a list of vital questions so you don't forget any important issues. Bear in mind, however, that you will be given an allotted amount of time. For more urgent or in-depth matters phone the school or drop a note in asking to see a particular teacher after school.

- Need to make a point or a complaint? Resist picking up the phone in the heat of the moment as you may end up ranting. Instead, writing a letter will help you to think your point through calmly and present it clearly, as well as giving the school an opportunity to consider its reaction.

- Your child is getting into trouble at school? Talk to his teachers as soon as possible to find ways of improving behaviour. Also make sure your child knows that persistent negative behaviour may lead to exclusion which can affect future educational and job prospects.

Friendships

- With younger children, encourage friendships by inviting friends home for tea.

- As your child gets older, especially in the teen years, welcome all his friends to your house, even those you aren't keen on. You're more likely to find out what's going on in his life if he's happy to bring friends home.

- If you are not happy about a particular friendship, keep your feelings to yourself. Firstly, letting him know what you think will undermine his confidence in his choices, and secondly your disapproval may cause him to hang on more determinedly to that particular friendship.

- If you have a good reason for not liking a friend – you think, for example, she or he is a bad influence – make sure lines of communication are kept wide open and that your child knows he can talk to you without being judged. Chances are he'll have a sense that this isn't the best kind of friendship, and feeling free to talk to you will help give him the courage to trusts his own instincts.

- With older children, take problems or friendship break-ups seriously. Offer advice and support but otherwise don't get involved.

- Leave your children to sort out friendship problems for themselves. Young children especially make and break friends frequently. Saying anything negative about his 'friend' may make it harder for him to 'make up' at a later date. Offer sympathy and advice but don't get involved.

- Accept that you can't choose your child's friends. If you don't like his chosen mates, avoid being openly critical as your child is more likely to jump to their defence.

- Encourage friendships outside of school. This will give your child the chance to relax away from the often intense relationships he has with friends he sees every day.

> *'If my daughter is upset at school, it's usually to do with one of her friendships. I've found the best thing to do is just listen a lot, and not worry too much. Within a few days the problem usually sorts itself out.'*
>
> Anna, mum to Chloe, aged ten

Bullying

Being bullied can deeply affect a child's self-confidence. Bullying itself can take many shapes and forms but essentially it's designed to hurt, either verbally or physically.

If your child is being bullied, he'll be frightened to go to school, and will look for reasons to stay at home, complaining perhaps of having a headache or tummy ache, which may be real or made up. You may notice a change in his behaviour – he may become negative and pessimistic, withdrawn or unusually argumentative. He'll find it hard to concentrate and his schoolwork may deteriorate. Depending on the nature of the bullying you may also find he's stealing from you or that his belongings are getting damaged or mysteriously disappearing.

- Listen carefully. If you suspect your child is being bullied, give him a chance to talk to you. Don't trivialise what he says. Believe him, and don't allow others to belittle his accounts.

- Stay calm. An over-reaction will frighten him and make him feel the situation is beyond his control.

- Discuss ways he might be able to sort out the problem himself. Dealing with it on his own will help him regain his confidence.

- If you can't see a way to resolve the problem, contact the school as soon as possible – don't wait until parents' evening. Schools today are legally obliged to have an anti-bullying policy and should take the situation seriously.

- If you are unhappy with the school's reaction contact the school's board of governors and local education authority.

- Don't let him take the blame. Explain that the problem lies with the bully, not with him.

- Take any threats of suicide seriously and get professional help straightaway (see Further Sources of Information, page 153).

- Find ways to rebuild your child's confidence. Encourage dependable friendships and outside interests so he can make new friends.

Summary of Chapter 11

- Education starts at home. The key is to make learning fun, within your child's ability range and part of everyday life.
- When choosing a school, look for one that's right for your child, not right for you.
- Keep track of what goes on at school by getting involved through the PTA, meeting other parents and chatting to your child.
- Encourage good homework habits, take an interest in your child's work and offer support and advice whenever possible.
- Value all your child's achievements, not just academic success.
- Support your child's friendships, encourage him to sort out problems for himself and offer advice without judging him.
- Watch out for signs that your child is being bullied and take the possibility seriously. If your child can't deal with it himself, get the school involved as soon as possible.

CHAPTER 12

Your Healthy, Happy Child

For you these are the golden years. Once your child starts school, she will become increasingly independent, freeing you from the tiring physical chores that took up so much time when she was younger. But at the same time her growing individuality, blossoming interest in the world around her, natural creativity and infectious enthusiasm make her fun to be with.

Family weekends and holidays offer great opportunities for building memories: you no longer have to organise the day around naps or mealtimes and your child is more flexible and can cope with a change in routine. And from her first meal in a Chinese restaurant to body surfing on holiday, she'll relish every new experience.

As the years progress, school and friends will become increasingly important, but for now, from hugs and kisses to sharing confidences and having good times together, you and your family play a central role in your child's life.

Keeping your child healthy and happy during these years means helping her develop more independence and a sense of responsibility. As she naturally demands more control over her life, helping her to maintain a healthy lifestyle (well-balanced meals, regular exercise and plenty of sleep) may become more challenging but with some creative thought you can still do much to promote her physical well-being.

Making sure she has plenty of time to play is also vital. Whether it's messing around with friends or amusing herself, having the means and opportunities to play will not only help her develop a whole range of skills but also give her the chance to develop interests and passions that will add to her enjoyment and pleasure in life – not just now but perhaps for many years to come.

Learning to enjoy healthy food

As your child spends more time eating outside the house (school lunch, tea with friends, parties, sleepovers) she's bound to discover what you might consider 'unhealthy' foods, and you won't necessarily be on hand to influence her choices.

At this age your child needs to feel she fits in with the crowd, and it would be unfair to expect her to say no to the occasional bag of crisps or chicken nuggets and chips. But that's not to say it's pointless encouraging her to think about what goes into her food, about what's healthy and what's not. Even if she has the odd lapse, your attitudes will continue to influence her, and help her make the right decisions for her own health as she moves into adolescence and then adulthood when it's much easier to keep up good habits than break bad ones.

So what is a healthy diet at this age? Pretty much the same as it is for an adult – low-fat, high-fibre foods with moderate salt and sugar; plenty of carbohydrates (bread, cereals and potatoes), five portions of fruit and vegetables plus a few servings of dairy products (including milk and alternatives) and protein (meat, fish and alternatives) each day. Sugary, fatty foods should be kept to a minimum.

A wide variety of foods eaten in these proportions will also help your child maintain a healthy weight. Obesity is a significant issue in the western world, and one that governments are taking increasingly seriously due to its health implications, including increased risk of premature death, diabetes and heart disease as well as severe back pain and other joint problems. In the UK around one in four two- to three-year-olds are either overweight or obese, and an obese seven-year-old has a 41 per cent chance of becoming an obese adult.

Of course, there can be a huge gap between presenting your child with food that's good for her, and actually getting her to clear the plate. While some will wolf down everything you put in front of them, others develop inexplicable likes and dislikes, and treat anything new with at best suspicion and at worst disdain. Naturally, watching your child turn her nose up at the food you've prepared can be infuriating.

So how can you get your child interested in sharing the same healthy and wide-ranging foods that you enjoy?

Wax lyrical about 'real' food

You might not persuade your child that something is worth eating because it's good for her, but getting excited about the way it tastes – 'Mmm, these flapjacks are so crunchy' or 'This melon is deliciously juicy' – may help to get the message across.

Dish the dirt on junk food

Grab every chance you can to say how horrible something tastes because it's so greasy or sugary or artificial tasting. Show your child how to read labels; she'll love spotting e-numbers for herself. Explain why some foods are bad for you.

Eat together

Family meals are the best place for children to learn about good food. If your child sees you and other family members enjoying their food, she is more likely to give something new a try. Even if you can't all eat together every day, a family meal a couple of times a week or at weekends can really help.

Don't offer alternatives

Try to make sure there's always something offered at mealtimes that you know your child likes. Then, if she turns her nose up at the food, you can accept a compromise – 'You don't like the fish? But you like potatoes and carrots so if you're going to leave the fish you'll need to eat a few mouthfuls of those.' Get your child used to the fact that if she won't eat what everyone else is having she'll have to go without as there's nothing else on offer. Meanwhile, she won't starve. If she asks for a snack before the next meal, offer her a piece of fruit or glass of water. Being consistent will help her to realise that you won't give in to demands for snacks.

Experiment

Children love new experiences, and eating out offers a great opportunity to tempt your child to try something different. Avoid chain restaurants and child-friendly pubs that only offer kids' menus. Instead, try your local neighbourhood for Italian, Indian, Chinese or Spanish restaurants. If you go at lunchtime they will probably welcome children, and you can ask if they will do half portions if your child isn't up to eating a full-sized meal.

Keep sugary foods for mealtimes only

It's the frequency, rather than the quantity, of sugar that leads to tooth decay in children. Sweet foods and drinks are less likely to be damaging if they are only eaten at mealtimes.

Offer healthy snacks

Growing children inevitably get peckish between meals, especially when they get home from school or if they are going through a growth spurt. The best way to ensure they eat only healthy snacks is to avoid having biscuits or crisps in the house. Instead encourage your child to have a cracker with cream cheese, chopped fresh raw fruit, vegetable sticks or bread sticks with hummus, mashed banana on toasted fingers. These release energy slowly and will help to avoid mood swings caused by yo-yoing blood sugar levels.

'I often ask my children to look through the cook books and choose something they like the look of. If they've decided what we're eating, they are much more likely to make an effort to eat it up.'

Eileen, mum to Ben, aged eight, and Samuel, aged six

Making exercise a habit

Even if you are a natural couch potato, your child needs to be active. Getting her up on her feet and into action will help her to develop a healthy heart and strong muscles and bones, and to reduce body fat. It will also improve her mood and help her to sleep better. Watch her rush in after an afternoon playing ball in the park, with rosy cheeks and a smile on her face, and later crash into bed.

Most importantly, like healthy eating, getting your child into good habits now will help her keep fit and well in later life. Research has shown that physically active children are more likely to remain active in later life. And adults who are fit are less likely to develop serious illnesses such as heart disease, diabetes and osteoporosis.

So how much exercise does a growing child need? Studies show that to maintain the right level of fitness, children should be having at least one hour's exercise of 'moderate intensity' a day. This could include activities such as fast walking, swimming, cycling, dance, games like chase, and most sports. Weight-bearing exercises, such as climbing, skipping, jumping and gymnastics are especially beneficial as they naturally maintain muscle strength, flexibility and bone health.

Getting this amount of exercise shouldn't be too hard. Walking briskly to school and back most days, for example, charging about in the playground, a couple of PE lessons and a regular activity such as football or swimming plus a family outing at the weekend can easily add up to an average of one hour a day.

Even if your child isn't naturally sporty, it's important to encourage her to be active. Besides helping her maintain her fitness, being even reasonably competent at an activity will boost her confidence. Joining in with other children has lots of social benefits as well as teaching her about fair play and give and take. And any new skills she learns now can be used in later life to meet people and have fun. Here are some ideas on how to encourage your child to get active:

- Think in terms of health and fitness rather than organised games. This helps to expand the range of activities your child might be interested in, from the obvious like football and tennis to the less common like ice-skating and judo.

- Let her try anything she seems even vaguely interested in. This needn't be expensive. If, for example she loves watching tennis, borrow a few rackets and hire a local court for an hour or so; alternatively, take advantage of the fact that lots of clubs run taster sessions for beginners.

- Get a friend involved too. Often it's the prospect of standing out because she's 'new' that puts a child off starting an activity. Joining with a friend has the added bonus of shared responsibility for picking up and dropping off at the venue.

- If she's keen but worried about her lack of experience, you might consider paying for a few private lessons to boost her confidence.

- Bear in mind your child's personality when helping her to find an activity that she likes. Outgoing children often enjoy more competitive team sports, so look for games like netball, hockey, basketball, football, rugby; others who are less assertive may find activities where they can progress at their own speed, like swimming or pony riding, more enjoyable.

- If she needs lots of encouragement, ease her in slowly. Let her go along and watch first, and meet the coach. Stay with her until she feels happy to be left, and give her lots of praise, keeping the feedback positive and avoiding pushing her too hard. The emphasis should always be on enjoyment, rather than achievement.

> *'Agnes isn't at all competitive but after playing badminton in the garden one summer, she agreed to join a badminton club with a friend. As long as there's no pressure to get involved in matches she's happy to play just for the fun of it.'*
>
> Isobella, mum to Agnes, aged nine

- Get the whole family involved. Younger children especially find almost any activity more appealing if their parents are involved too. Seeing that you attach value to physical activity will help her to see it as worthwhile. Good weekend family activities include swimming, cycling, ice-skating and walking.

Finding time for play

As your child gets older, play should still be an important part of her life. Whether it's building a den in the sitting room, putting together a show with friends, or going off exploring on her bike, play time is not only relaxing for your child, but stimulating too. It gives her the chance to discover new ways to solve a problem, for example, or uncover talents and skills she never knew she had.

With hectic schedules (yours and hers), easy distractions like television and computer games, and a tendency to keep little ones indoors where they are safe from traffic, opportunities for children to discover the pleasure of play can become few and far between. The following suggestions can help to ensure that your child still has the chance to play.

- Don't over-schedule your child's life. Having plenty of free time will give her the chance to explore her own interests and develop new passions.

- Don't worry about her getting bored. Boredom is the best way for her to discover how to be resourceful.

- Be supportive when your child shows an interest in a new pastime. This needn't mean shelling out lots of money. Just being prepared to listen when she talks to you and understand why it excites her will show that you take it seriously.

- If the computer or television seems to rule her free time, set some firm limits. A kitchen timer is a great way of keeping a check on how she's using her time.

- If you are concerned about your child playing outdoors without you nearby to watch over her, try to get out at weekends and on holiday so she can go bike riding, climb trees and have some sense of freedom.

'My eleven-year-old still loves to muck in with her younger brothers. They'll dress up together and make films with the video camera, get all the Lego out and create mini worlds, or spend hours over a board game.'

Penny, mum to Sophie, aged 11, Zac, aged nine, and Patrick, aged seven

Fostering independence

One of your most important aims should be to help your child become a capable adult. As she gets older, she'll naturally want to do things for herself, and she should be allowed to. Unfortunately, it's so easy to get used to doing things for your child, that sometimes you don't notice when she is capable of managing on her own. You're still pouring out her drink and buttoning up her coat while she's wanting to visit the shops or go to the park on her own.

You may also carry on doing things for your child because you think it's quicker or less messy. But then you find yourself complaining when she appears incapable of picking up toys after herself, hanging the towel back properly on the rail or putting her school shoes in the cupboard.

Encouraging your child to become more independent is essential for her healthy emotional development (and often has the added benefit of helping you along the way). Being asked to do a 'grown-up' job, for example, will boost your child's sense of self-esteem: you're telling your child you trust her, and think she is capable. And letting your child make her own choices, within appropriate parameters, will help her to think about the relationship between action and consequences, while at the same time giving her a valuable sense of responsibility.

Learning that independence and responsibility go hand in hand will help your child at all stages of her life as she grows and develops. Deciding, for example, that she's old enough to care for a pet of her own means she has to take responsibility for making sure the animal is regularly fed and watered. Being given a room of her own means taking on responsibility for keeping it tidy.

Having the freedom to go to the park without you means remembering to come home at the agreed hour.

The process of encouraging independence should already have started: tidying up after getting her toys out, washing her own face, etc. From the age of about eight your child is likely to strive for more and more independence and this requires a considered response from you as a parent.

- As your child gets older, steadily allow her increased freedom and responsibility. Doing everything for her, then suddenly letting go will leave her without the skills she needs to cope.

- Deal with each request for more independence on its own merit. For example, are other children doing this sort of thing? Can I trust her? Are there steps that should be taken first before reaching this point?

- Don't thrust responsibility on a child who isn't ready for it. Her friends may be getting the bus into town but perhaps she needs to do it with you a few times before trying it for herself.

- Strike a balance between independence and rules. As your child grows she needs to know that her choices and freedoms are acceptable within certain limits (see Chapter 13, page 109) and that these limits are important for everyone to live happily within the family.

- A child who is naturally unsure of herself may feel nervous about making the 'wrong' decision, or not being able to cope with a task she has been given. Help by encouraging her to do things easily within her capabilities at first, then as she gets more confident she can try more challenging tasks.

'My son and daughter are very different. Joey was desperate to do things on his own – like go across the road to the shop – from a very young age. Katy is much more of a worrier and although she's two years older is only now beginning to want to be more independent.'

Elaine, mum to Joey, aged eight, and Katy, aged ten

Nurturing positive values

Once your child starts school, her peer group will have an increasing effect on her ideas and attitudes about people and relationships, and this influence may cause conflict between you. Sometimes she may be encouraged to do things that she instinctively feels are wrong, or that make her uncomfortable.

Helping your child develop, and feel confident about her own moral judgement will make it easier for her to resist being influenced by the crowd and to stand by her own values and beliefs.

You can help your child develop her moral judgement in a number of ways.

● Talk about the way people behave, in stories, films and at school. This offers lots of opportunities to discuss in a way your child can understand what makes people act as they do.

● Be open about your own values. Explain why, for example, you disapprove of lying, cheating, dropping litter, shoplifting or racism and approve of politeness, fair play, table manners, etc.

● Show her in the way you interact with other people that everyone (whatever their sex, religion or ethnicity) deserves to be treated with politeness and respect.

● Give your child the chance to express her own opinions. They may be different to yours, they may change as the months go by, but being given an opportunity to think about, value and express her own opinions and judgements will help her to develop a strong idea of who she is.

● Get into the habit of naming emotions ('You look angry', 'Your sister's crying because she's sad', 'You've made me cross') so that your child can recognise how other people are feeling, and take responsibility for the impact her behaviour can have.

SUMMARY OF CHAPTER 12

These are the golden years. Your child is becoming increasingly capable and independent, yet still loves your company, and relishes being part of the family.

- Keep encouraging healthy eating habits. You might not always have control over what she eats now, but being clear about what's good to eat and what's not will influence her choices.

- Help her to find a physical activity she enjoys. Growing children need at least one hour of moderate exercise a day to keep fit and healthy.

- Don't over-schedule your child's life. Play is still important and she needs enough free time to get bored, and then discover how to entertain herself.

- Although you still play a central role in your child's life, over the years to come she'll need, and demand, more independence. Steadily encouraging her to become more capable will boost her confidence and sense of responsibility.

- Nurture positive values and help your child to develop her own moral judgement by being open about your own, showing by example and letting your child have her own opinions.

CHAPTER 13

Managing Behaviour

Encouraging your child to behave well, to be truthful and polite, as well as cooperative, kind and helpful, benefits everyone. Family life runs more smoothly, your child develops the social skills he needs to make friends, and he's able to get along well in school and in life generally.

So how do children discover what's okay and what's not when it comes to behaviour? In a number of ways: through your positive reactions (when he does something you like, you give him lots of praise and attention); through imitation (how you behave towards him and how you interact with your partner and your friends); and through discipline (how you enforce rules and standards of behaviour).

Getting the best out of your child

Children are born wanting to please. Just think about your tiny newborn, and how he learns to smile. One day he copies you, and then sensing your pleasure he learns that smiling is a good thing. Building on this natural instinct will help to instil the value of good behaviour from an early age and help you to get the best out of your child.

- Always find opportunities to praise your child for good behaviour, and do it immediately. This is especially important with younger children. If, for example, he asks nicely for the jam at the breakfast table, say 'Well done for remembering your please and thank you' as this will help him to see the connection between what he has done and your positive attention.

- Show your appreciation with rewards and privileges. If, for example, your 12-year-old offers to run over to the shop to get that extra pint of milk, ask if he'd like to do something fun with you afterwards like playing his favourite board game or staying up to watch a television programme.

- Ignore minor misdemeanours whenever you can. Children frequently like to be irritating just to get their parents' attention, and constantly nagging or disciplining not only helps them to achieve their aim, but also creates a negative mood. Instead, pretend you haven't noticed, so that it's no longer in your child's interest to continue being annoying.

- Distract or redirect your child. The behaviour of young children especially can be managed in this way. If, for example, you know your youngest always wants whichever toy his older sister has chosen to play with, be ready with something equally interesting to grab his attention.

> 'It was my mother who pointed out how down I was on Will. He's quite a cheeky little boy and, as she said, I only seemed to speak to him when he needed telling off, which is quite often! I've since tried harder to look for the good things he does, and make sure I tell him when I'm pleased. I can't say he's now an angel, but he is trying harder to be good.'
>
> Tricia, mum to Will, aged eight

Setting clear limits and boundaries

Your child can only behave well when he's clear what is expected of him, and this means you need to make sure he knows what is and isn't allowed and exactly what the limits are.

Some boundaries you choose to set will be age specific. Young children, for example, need boundaries to keep them safe ('You can't cross the road unless I'm holding your hand'). Older children need limits to help them learn to be fair ('Everyone deserves a piece of cake, so it must be shared out equally'), considerate ('You need to ring me when you arrive at your friend's house so I know you are safe') and responsible ('Having your own room is a privilege and I expect you to keep it tidy yourself').

Make it easier for your child to stick within the limits with a few simple strategies.

● Establish routines. Spend a few days repeatedly reminding your child (just saying it once or twice may not be enough) to make his bed first thing in the morning, hang his coat up as soon as he comes in or do his homework before watching television, and these habits will quickly become ingrained.

● Be consistent. Once you've established a rule (bed at nine, piano practice before play or ask before using the phone) stick with it. There will be plenty of occasions when your child begs for flexibility but if you give in once, it'll become increasingly hard to stick to your guns in the future.

● Review the rules as your child grows up. What's right for a toddler isn't necessarily right for a seven-year-old. And as children develop more independence, it's important that they are given as much freedom as possible within reasonable limits.

● Involve your child in decision-making. Although you should always have the final say, your child needs to know that his opinions count. And being given the chance to question, discuss and demand reasons and explanations will help him to accept the final decision.

> *'My youngest caught me out the other day. He knows he's not allowed biscuits before bedtime but he wouldn't stop waving the tin in front of me while I was on the phone. I foolishly nodded in agreement, just so he'd leave me alone, and now he thinks he's allowed a biscuit every night!'*
>
> Sandra, mum to Alfie, aged ten

Reacting fairly

All children get it wrong sometimes. Younger ones often simply 'forget' that, for example, they've been asked not to run inside the house with muddy shoes, to flush the loo after using it or to eat with a knife and fork, not their fingers.

Older children want to feel as if they, not you, are in control of their lives, and try to assert themselves by lounging in front of the television instead of getting on with their homework, spending their lunch money on crisps and chocolate rather than a hot meal, and using the phone to call a friend without checking first that it's okay.

Often you can find yourself taking on the role of a metaphorical punchball. Your child has had an argument with a friend, is overtired and grumpy, feels you haven't been paying him much attention recently or has had a bad day at school. Taking his frustration and fury out on you is a safe bet – he knows you won't hold it against him – but can be difficult for you to cope with.

Whatever the offence, it's important to react fairly. After all, the purpose of disciplining children is to help them see the consequences of their actions, and encourage them to behave better next time.

- Try to stay calm and kind but firm. Your child will understand your point of view better if he can focus on what you are saying rather than how you are saying it. Although it's natural to feel angry when your child has behaved badly, speaking harshly will upset him, and make him naturally defensive.

- Think before you speak. A rush of anger can result in a bad choice of words or an inappropriate punishment. If your emotions are running so high you fear you can't act calmly, ask your child to go his room until you are ready to talk to him about the issue.

- If you do blow a fuse, and it's inevitable that there will be times when this happens, apologise as quickly as you can, and explain to your child that you reacted badly, you were tired or had had a bad day. Don't blame him for your anger.

Seeing you take responsibility for your emotions will help him learn how to control his own.

● Be realistic. All children make mistakes, and small mistakes sometimes need only be pointed out.

● If you feel discipline of some form is necessary (see page 113) check that it's appropriate for your child's age, personality and the seriousness of the offence.

● Avoid making your child feel guilty. If you explain clearly and firmly to your child why you are upset, he is more likely to understand your point of view. Holding a grudge will simply leave him feeling hopeless, resentful and less motivated to change his behaviour.

'Occasionally, especially when I'm tired, I get very snappy with the girls – but I always apologise afterwards. Now, if one of them gets in a fury and yells at me, they usually say sorry later, which I really appreciate.'

Cate, mum to Stephanie and Emily, both aged 12

Resolving disagreements

Families bicker and argue – it's a fact of life. Only the issues will vary, depending on your child's age, stage and personality. Sometimes the disagreements will be minor – your child wants a biscuit but tea is nearly ready so the answer is no. He knows the family rules are no snacking between meals, so that should be the end of the argument. Sometimes, however, disagreements will arise over issues you may not yet have had the chance to tackle. For example, your child doesn't feel like going to his piano lesson tonight, or your teenager has planned a sleepover without checking with you first.

Learning to resolve disagreements effectively with minimum tears and tantrums (from you and your child!) is important not only for maintaining your relationship with your child but also for teaching him skills that he will be able to use throughout his life.

- Remember that finding a solution you can both live with is more important than winning the battle. Trying to prove that you are right and your child is wrong can blow an argument out of all proportion.

- Identify the problem. It can be all too easy to over-react and blow up over side issues that have nothing to do with the central disagreement. Let your child explain freely, without interruption, exactly what the problem is – 'I don't want to go to my piano lesson because I didn't practise this week' or 'I've already invited my friends for the sleepover. It'll be so embarrassing telling them they can't come.'

- Voice your child's feelings – 'You are upset because…', 'You feel that…' – so that your child knows you understand his point of view.

- Explain your point of view – 'Even if you haven't done your practice it's still worth going', 'Checking beforehand about sleepovers gives me the chance to make arrangements so your fun doesn't impinge on the rest of the family.'

- Work together to try to solve the problem. Brainstorm ideas that would be acceptable to you both, even though you both may have to compromise. For example, perhaps your child could say to his piano teacher that he's been very busy this week and hasn't been able to do as much practice as normal, and maybe your teenager could have a sleepover but next week rather than this week.

Enforcing discipline

However hard you try to be positive and encourage good behaviour, to respond fairly when they make mistakes, and to resolve disagreements, there will be occasions (for some children few, for others many) when you need to act to make it clear that what your child did is unacceptable and won't be tolerated.

A generation or so ago, smacking was seen as an acceptable way of disciplining a child. Nowadays, most parents accept the research that shows smacking does nothing to help children learn how to improve their behaviour. In fact, all it does is confuse a child who has been taught that physical violence (biting a sister, hitting a friend) is unacceptable.

Today's less punitive attitude to discipline, does, however, have its own problems. No parent wants to damage their relationship with their child, and for some this can make saying 'no' difficult. But when it comes to showing your child that his actions have consequences, being a great mum means being prepared to be unpopular at times.

Stay calm

Unless you've had the chance to calm down and think about the situation rationally and objectively, it's impossible to discipline your child fairly, in a way that will allow him to learn from the experience.

Tell your child what he has done wrong

Although often your child may be quite clear about his misbehaviour, there may be times when he is genuinely confused about why he is in trouble.

Explain why his behaviour is not acceptable

This may be because it was dangerous, hurtful, rude or provocative. If your child is capable, ask him to think about and explain the consequences of his actions.

Decide on the appropriate level of discipline

This should be done calmly and rationally and should be judged on the severity of the 'offence', whether it was committed without thinking, or whether it has been committed repeatedly and deliberately. Here are some suggestions.

- **A verbal warning.** Ask your child not to repeat his behaviour and remind him that if he does, the punishment will be more severe. This gives your child the chance to behave properly.

- **Making amends.** If your child has upset someone, he needs to find a way of making that person feel better. If he ran across the floor with muddy feet he can wipe up the mess. This can, for example, prove the point that it's often less hassle to avoid misbehaving in the first place.

- **Time out.** Send your child out of the room for a period of time. This can give your child the chance to calm down and think about what he has done. This may be more suitable for younger children.

- **Banning treats and/or privileges.** Take away something your child loves (sweets, television, computer, pocket money, going out with friends, having friends round) for a couple of days, a week or longer. It can also help to ask your child a few questions at the end of the ban period, such as, 'Do you remember why your behaviour was inappropriate?' or 'Can I trust you not to misbehave in this way again?'

> *'I really hate punishing the children, but I realise that setting limits now will make life easier for all of us as they get older. My sister has a fairly unruly teenager who's always pretty much had his own way, and finds it very hard to accept discipline from anyone – his parents and teachers.'*
>
> Peggy, mum to Zara, aged nine, and Jacob, aged six

SUMMARY OF CHAPTER 13

Encouraging your child to behave will help him get along at home, in school and in life generally.

- Try to get the best out of your child with lots of praise and appreciation when he behaves well.
- Set clear limits and boundaries so it's clear what's expected of him.
- React fairly when your child makes a mistake, or does something wrong.
- Make finding a solution to disagreements, rather than winning the battle, your priority.
- Be prepared to be unpopular at times. There will inevitably be occasions when you have to discipline your child.

CHAPTER 14

Your Healthy, Happy Teenager

In many ways the teen years start when your child makes the move from primary to secondary school. Suddenly she's surrounded by older children and all the influences and issues that come with them. She needs to be more responsible and motivated, while at the same time she's facing some of the biggest physical and emotional changes she'll ever have to deal with.

Many parents look ahead at the prospect of having a teenager in the house and shudder – and not surprisingly, as the teenage years are typically portrayed as a time of tension and conflict. But while it's inevitable that at times the huge changes your teenager is experiencing will affect her moods and sensitivity, life doesn't have to be a constant round of slammed doors, arguments and huffs. With a loving and stable home life, most teenagers (and their parents) get through this period unscathed, and mature into happy and caring young people.

'I realised the teen years were going to be hard on both of us unless I really tried to understand what she was going through. It isn't always easy, but I think we've reached the stage where I can trust her to be sensible and she knows I'm here if she needs to talk.'

Miriam, mum to Martha, aged 15

The key to helping your teenager stay on an even keel lies in understanding and supporting her. She may increasingly look like an adult, but she is still in many ways a child, and still incredibly naïve. She needs to be handled with understanding and sensitivity, to be accepted for who she is and, while maintaining reasonable limits and boundaries, gently allowed some independence.

Encouraging your child to keep fit and healthy

Puberty brings with it a whole range of physical and emotional changes. And the impact of hormones, growth spurts and anxieties about appearance, friendship and schoolwork can all take their toll on your child's health. Encouraging her to eat well, get plenty of sleep and take exercise will give her the physical resources she needs to cope. This is also the age when the 'big' issues of sex, smoking, drugs and alcohol have to be dealt with, and helping her stay safe depends on keeping the channels of communication open.

Diet

- Your child is growing fast and needs extra calories (more than an adult) to keep up her energy levels, so don't be surprised if she's always starving when she gets home from school or still hungry after a meal. Keep lots of healthy snacks on hand (see Chapter 12, page 100) so she doesn't resort to crisps and fizzy drinks.

- Once periods start, girls need lots of iron to replace menstrual losses and keep their energy levels up, so include plenty of high-iron foods in your child's diet, such as broccoli, raisins, watermelon and chickpeas. Vitamin C is necessary to absorb iron so she'll need to have a glass of orange juice, for example, with the meal.

- Both boys and girls need extra calcium to keep up with the rapid increase in bone mass. Boys need to aim for about 1000mg a day, girls about 800mg. As a guide, a cup of full-fat milk contains about 300mg of calcium.

- Food may become an issue for your teenager if she feels stressed or unhappy. If she occasionally eats too little or over-indulges, don't let it worry you, but if it carries on for an extended period, your teenager may be using the control of food as a way to deal with difficulties in her life. Although most common in girls, boys can be affected too, so if you think your teenager may have an eating disorder such as anorexia or bulimia, seek advice from your GP.

Exercise

- Exercise is not just good for your teenager's health, it will lift her mood as well (see Dealing with mood swings, page 123). Motivate her into action by explaining the feel-good factor of being active.

- Don't be a chauffeur. She's old enough to get herself around, and will get more exercise if she walks or cycles to school, the shops or her friends' houses.

- If your teenager is reluctant to take exercise, encourage her to try activities that are sociable and she can enjoy with her friends, like badminton, tennis, swimming or cycle rides.

Sleep

- Explain to your teenager that she ought to be having at least nine hours sleep a night. Deep sleep is vital to help her grow and develop properly, and research has shown that children who don't sleep well may not grow well.

- Try to be flexible about sleep patterns. If she's done her homework and chores, is it really a problem if she stays in bed until lunchtime on a Sunday?

- Encourage her to take responsibility for getting to bed and getting up in the morning. If she's tired during the day or late for school, she'll quickly work out that she needs to get to bed earlier and set her alarm clock before she goes to sleep.

Sex

It can be hard recognising that your child is developing into a sexual being. But for your teenager, thinking about sex, wanting sex and, at some point, having sex is inevitable. According to research, however, your teenager is more likely to wait before having sex for the first time and be more sensible about protection against unwanted pregnancy and sexually transmitted infections (STIs) if she is properly informed.

Although children are given sex education at school, and can find out a lot by reading magazines and chatting to their friends, research also shows that the person they really want to hear it from is you. Being able to talk about sexual relationships with your teenager may not always feel natural or easy, but overcoming your embarrassment will help to keep her safe, and will mean she is more likely to feel confident about coming to you when she needs advice or help.

- Try to be relaxed and open on the subject, even though you may find this embarrassing. The more straightforward you are, the less mystery there will be for your teenager.

- Be realistic. Let her know that sex isn't always as passionate and torrid as the media likes to suggest, that the giving and taking of pleasure takes time to learn, and that the right time to start a sexual relationship is when she feels certain she's ready (although it is important to point out too that the legal age is 16).

- Make sure she understands the mechanics and risks of sex.

- Talk about contraception. Bear in mind that while the pill protects against unwanted pregnancy, condoms are the only way to protect against common sexually transmitted diseases such as chlamydia (especially prevalent among teenagers), herpes, gonorrhoea and HIV.

- Your son may find it less embarrassing to learn about sex and using contraception from his father, so suggest a one-to-one session. As back-up, there are plenty of good sex education books available and useful leaflets. Look in your GP's waiting room.

- There is a lot of information for your child to take on board, so rather than just having one major discussion and hoping it all sinks in, try to use any appropriate moments to talk about the subject.

- If you feel your child is concerned about sexual issues but too embarrassed to talk to you, check out your bookshop for a book written on the subject for this age group and leave it around for her to look at privately.

'I use TV programmes, such as the soaps, to discuss issues such as unwanted pregnancy. My daughter seems to find it easier to understand the consequences when she can relate it to a TV character!'

Siobhan, mum to Georgia, aged 15

Alcohol, drugs and smoking

These can be a fact of life for many teenagers today.

- Try to avoid lecturing your child about these issues. Instead make the point that your main concern is her health, safety and well-being.

- As with all types of peer pressure, being able to say 'no' depends to a huge extent on your child feeling secure in herself (see Boosting confidence, page 122).

- Let your younger teenager have her first taste of alcohol at home and make sure she is fully aware of the risks to her personal safety related to drinking too much (losing control, vomiting in her sleep). With older teenagers be realistic and make sure they know how to drink without getting drunk (drinking lots of water, not mixing drinks, having something to eat first).

- Schools provide lots of information on drugs. Read the material yourself so you are properly informed, and check that your teenager properly understands it too, including the risks and dangers, and how the law stands.

- If you discover your teenager has tried smoking or drugs, resist flying off the handle. This is the best way of making sure you never find out if it happens again. Remind yourself that trying is not the same as being addicted, then let your child explain how and why it happened.

- If you feel your teenager needs professional help, seek it out as soon as possible (see Further Sources of Information, page 153).

Boosting confidence

Confidence is important throughout life but especially so for teenagers. Puberty can be embarrassing and confusing, and even the most self-assured child can become a self-conscious and uncertain teen. She'll probably feel immense pressure from her peers to fit in – have the same hairstyle, wear the same clothes and listen to the same band. Being accepted as part of the gang helps your child feel good about herself at a time of uncertainty and insecurity. But sometimes this need to fit in may put pressure on your child to do things she's not happy about. Having a strong sense of herself, and good self-esteem, will help her be less dependent on her peer group for approval, and make it easier for her to resist the pressure to do things she's not sure about.

- Encourage her whenever possible to make her own choices and decisions. This doesn't mean you can't guide her with advice and suggestions but being able to think what's best for her will give her a stronger sense of self-worth.

- Listen to her opinions and ideas. Even if you don't agree with her, taking her thoughts seriously will make her feel she's valued.

- Try not to argue. When you have a dispute with your teenager, give her the chance to say her bit before saying yours. Two-way communication rather than an 'I'm right and you're wrong' row will help her feel she's being taken seriously.

- Try to balance criticism with praise. She might drive you mad for not keeping her room tidy, leaving the milk out or forgetting her lunch box, but a few positive comments will make it easier for her to take on board the negative ('I love the way you've decorated your wall. Would you tidy up your clothes now?').

● Use descriptive praise to build her self-esteem. Rather than a 'that's great', tell her why you think it's great ('Thanks for taking out the rubbish. I'm really pushed for time today and that helped a lot' or 'That's a super piece of work. I can see you had to do a lot of research').

● Don't compare her unfavourably with her peers. Emphasise that doing her best is what counts, not how well she measures up against her friends.

● Find opportunities to treat her like an adult. Ask her to book the tickets for the cinema or choose something for supper at the supermarket.

● Don't be afraid to say no. Even though she may rage against you, setting limits and boundaries (see Chapter 13, page 109) shows her that you care, and makes her feel secure. And the more loved and valued she feels at home, the more confidence she'll have in the outside world.

> *'I love the fact that my son has the confidence to say, "Actually, Mum, I don't agree with you on that one." I enjoy listening to his ideas – at least he's got some!'*
>
> Serena, mum to Tom, aged 15

Dealing with mood swings

Emotional highs and lows are part of life for your growing teenager, and not surprisingly, when you think about what she is dealing with: turbulent hormones, peer pressure, mounting work at school, a changing body and a confused mind. Your child is half-way between being an adult and a child, at times mature and at others completely irrational. In short, her feelings are often all over the place.

But even though they may be normal, a teenager's mood

swings are not easy to live with, especially as there will be times when your teenager is also rude, argumentative and generally uncooperative. Maintaining your family's limits and boundaries on behaviour (see Chapter 13, page 109) will help keep the peace. Meanwhile, staying calm and supportive will help her to feel loved and secure and better able to handle her emotions.

- Like toddlers, teenagers are prone to grumpiness when their blood sugar levels are low, so when she's inexplicably short-tempered and irritable offer her something healthy to snack on – carbohydrates like bananas, potatoes and pasta are especially good.

- Regularly reassure her that if she's worried about something, or just wants to talk, you will always be there for her. Don't grill her, but make sure you have quiet times together when she can open up to you if she feels like it, for example when shopping together, in the car or over a meal.

- If your teenager does open up to you, let her see that you are really listening (see Chapter 15, page 131) by stopping what you are doing and giving your full attention (a common complaint from teenagers is that their parents never really listen!)

- Don't belittle any problems your teenager shares with you. Whether it's a break-up with a boyfriend, a falling-out with a friend or worries over her appearance, teenagers are very sensitive, and need to know that they are being taken seriously.

- Think before you speak. Choose your words carefully and don't be judgemental or angry. She's less likely to open up to you again if you over-react. Instead, focus on exploring together ways to deal with the problem.

- If your child stomps out screaming 'I'm leaving home', she probably just needs time to let off steam. Make sure you have her friends' mobile numbers so you can be reassured that she's okay, then try to stay calm when she comes back. Explain that you were worried because you didn't know where she was, then talk about the issue that caused the initial upset.

- If she's more often moody than not, look out for signs of depression such as constant crying, staying in her room all day, loss of interest in favourite activities, not looking after her appearance, sleeping a lot, avoiding contact with family and friends, self-harming or talking about suicide or death.

- Take any threats of suicide seriously. Talk to your GP about possible treatments, such as counselling or anti-depressants. Encourage your teenager to talk to you and let her know you are always there for her. If she feels she can't talk to you, suggest contacting a professional organisation such as Young Minds (see Further Sources of Information, page 153).

'My daughter has days when she feels really low. I tell her that sadness always has a beginning, a middle and an end, and that it will go. I've also encouraged her to note the times she feels down in a diary. Looking back reassures her that these feelings will evaporate.'

Carol, mum to Becky, aged nearly 14

Letting go

For lots of parents letting go is one of the hardest parts of parenting a teenager.

Your child wants to spend more and more time away from you and, naturally, you are fearful for her safety and well-being. At the same time your teenager is starting to think and choose for herself, and there will be times when you won't agree with her opinions, or won't like the decisions she makes.

Letting go can be frightening because it feels like letting go of the close bond that you have. But the harder you hang on to your teenager, trying to control her thoughts and actions, the harder she'll fight to break free. Instead, you have to learn to trust her, accept that she's her own person and, through a process of negotiation and trade-offs, allow her the freedom she needs to mature into a capable and independent young adult.

- Accept that as long as she isn't hurting herself or anyone else, she's entitled to make her own decisions and have her own views (and dress sense, and friends and music preference).

- Recognise her need for privacy, from knocking on her bedroom door before going in to not expecting her to share her every thought with you. Allowing her privacy shows that you respect her as an individual.

- Give new freedoms gradually, checking along the way that she understands that responsibility (staying in touch, getting home when she says she will, and so on) goes hand in hand with independence.

- Don't be over-protective. Your teenager needs to make mistakes, big and small, to learn, even if this means walking home in the rain because she's forgotten her bus fare or failing an exam because she hasn't worked hard enough.

- Make sure she's clear about the limits and boundaries. Increased freedom should be an earned privilege and if she breaks your trust by not, for example, getting home on time, she risks losing that privilege.

- Keep telling her that you love her. She may not always feel approachable, and she will probably prefer to spend most of her time with her friends, but you are still her rock, and reassuring her that you care will help her feel confident about turning to you when she needs help and support.

SUMMARY OF CHAPTER 14

The key to helping your teenager mature into a capable and independent young person is to try to understand and support her.

- Puberty brings with it a whole range of physical and emotional changes. Encouraging your teenager to eat well, get plenty of sleep and take exercise will help her to cope better.

- Now's the time when the 'big' issues of sex, smoking, drink and drugs need to be discussed. Avoid lecturing, keep lines of communication open, and make sure your teenager (and you) are properly informed.

- A lack of confidence will affect her self-esteem and make it harder for her to resist negative peer pressure. Find ways to boost her self-esteem and help her feel good about herself.

- Mood swings are normal for teenagers. Support her by letting her know you will always listen to any worries she has, by not being judgemental and by taking her worries seriously. Keep a look-out for signs of depression.

- Be prepared to let go. Your teenager needs the freedom to grow and be her own person.

CHAPTER 15

Loving Your Child

This sounds like common sense but children can't mind read, so how do they know not only that you love them, but that you love them unconditionally? Some mums are naturally open and warm, easily able to demonstrate their love with words and actions. But others, maybe because they were brought up this way themselves, are less demonstrative and more reserved, and perhaps need to make more of an effort to express their love.

Learning how to communicate your love for your child isn't just about saying 'I love you'. Your love is also expressed in the way you communicate with him, the way you make time for him, and the way you accept him. Making sure your child knows that he is not only loved, but loved unconditionally, is one of the best ways of ensuring his happiness.

'When my daughter was 14 I found loving her very hard. She wound me up. I'd get irritable and jump down her throat. I knew things could only get worse if I didn't sort them out. I tried to find things we could do together – we started having a regular night out at the cinema. And I looked for the good things she did – just praising her made me feel better, and made it easier for me to feel loving.'

Fran, mum to Jo, aged 17

Accepting your child for who he is

Learning to accept your child for who he is is essential to unconditional love. This means letting go of your own hopes and dreams and letting him find his own. It means not preaching a philosophy of perfection – after all, no child can be perfect. And it means allowing him his own views and his own likes and dislikes, even when they are at odds with your own. Accepting your child for who he is shows him that you love him no matter what, and while he knows there will always be a price to pay for behaving badly (a ticking off or a loss of privileges) he also knows that that price won't be your love for him.

Making your child feel special

Whether it's choosing a book you both enjoy and reading a chapter a night together, mucking about in the park or in the garden with a ball or baking a cake, doing something together tells your child you value his company, that you find it enjoyable, and that you care for him. Even on a day when time is short and the best you can manage is to put the washing aside and sit down with your child ('It's been a busy day, come and sit down with me for a few moments') you'll be making him feel special and loved.

Being physically affectionate

For babies, close physical contact, whether it's cuddling, stroking, kissing or rocking, is incredibly important. Your loving touch helps him feel safe and secure, calms him when he's fretful, and helps to develop a close and trusting bond between you both.

As your child becomes more physically independent, hugs and cuddles become more valuable for expressing warmth and tenderness. Lots of families use watching television or reading books together as an excuse for snuggling up on the sofa. And while no child should be forced to hug, regular spontaneous hugs, given just for the hell of it, when your child is relaxed and receptive, are lovely to receive.

During the teenage years, your child may naturally become more self-conscious, and shy away from physical contact. But while his body language might be saying 'Don't touch me', physical affection can help him to feel lovable and attractive.

While hugs may be rebuffed, a hand on his back or shoulder while you're chatting in the kitchen or a quick kiss at bedtime will secretly be appreciated.

Using positive body language

Sometimes it's not what you say but how you say it. Children are very intuitive, and tone of voice, gestures, facial expression and posture can all express as much as words when it comes to communicating love. Tiny babies, for example, will often be more unsettled if their mother is tense, anxious or distressed. Loom over a toddler and tell him 'no' with a furious face and a wagging finger and he'll burst into tears, not just because he can't have his way but also because he is scared.

Looking your child in the eye when you speak to him and keeping your body language open and welcoming will reassure your child that he is still loved, whatever it is that you need to say to him.

Setting limits and boundaries

It's easy to fall into the trap of thinking that by giving your child what he wants you are proving your love for him. But being indulgent and always giving in to a child's wishes, especially when they are unreasonable or inappropriate, can lead to confusion. For example, saying 'Yes, you can do what you like' is another way of saying 'I don't care'.

Being prepared instead to say 'no' gives your child clear boundaries and helps him to feel safe and supported. As long as he is allowed reasonable freedom within those limits ('No, you can't get down until you've eaten some vegetables, but you can choose whichever you prefer' or 'No, you can't stay up tonight and watch the film, but you can stay up later at the weekend'), he will be reassured that you have his best interests at heart.

Giving praise

Noticing when your child does something good, and praising him for it, is one of the most loving things you can do. And it doesn't have to be something earth shattering like passing a music exam or scoring a goal in the school football match. In fact, the things you choose to praise him for will say a lot about what you value in him. By showing your approval when he's kind to his younger brother, for example, or when he tries really hard at something he finds difficult, you are indicating what you think is important. Positive words can make a huge difference in building your child's self-esteem and prove to him that you think he's special.

Being a good listener

One of the best ways to communicate your love to your child is to listen to him. Attentive listening, giving your child your full attention and letting him speak without interrupting or judging, shows respect for your child, and helps to build self-esteem. It makes a child feel confident that his opinions, interests and thoughts are worth listening to. It encourages him to open up and communicate with you. And it is also one of the best ways of keeping in touch with your child and how he is developing, especially as he goes through the teenage years, when you are likely to be surprised by some of the changes taking place.

- Show that you are interested when he talks. Make eye contact (with smaller children this may mean getting down to their height), face him directly and lean in towards him.

- Be open. Don't cross your arms or hunch forward in an aggressive way. If your child feels judged before he even starts he'll clam up.

- Let him finish. Don't interrupt with your views or interpretations until he's had his say; if he dries up just ask a few open questions (What? Why? How?) to encourage him to carry on.

- Reflect back what you hear. You can do this by repeating

some of the words or phrases your child has used, or his last sentence, or by commenting on his emotional reactions – for example, 'You seem angry' – to show him that you understand what he's telling you.

- Be unshockable. Children often say things for effect, to test your reactions, and shrieking in horror might make him clam up.

Communicating openly

Open, honest communication helps your child to feel supported, understood and close to you. Children should be able to talk freely about what's bothering them, and about what makes them happy.

- Discuss everyday decisions with your child, whether it's choosing what to have for supper, which film to rent, or where to go on holiday. Inviting your child to contribute his thoughts and ideas, even when they can't be accommodated, will help him realise how important they are.

- Create opportunities for talking together. This is often easier with younger children as they naturally spend more time with their parents. As older children get more independent you may need to work harder to find opportunities, such as in the car or during family mealtimes.

- Always try to answer your child's questions. Sometimes these will be easy ('Why do cows like eating grass?'); sometimes they might be more difficult ('Why do you sound grumpy when Granny phones?') but sharing with your child an answer that is appropriate to his age and understanding will help him to understand the world, understand you, and to feel safe expressing his thoughts and ideas.

- Avoid preaching. If your child has asked a question, or you want to tell him something, it's important to share your point of view and the reasoning behind it without delivering a lecture. Preaching is simply telling a child what to do without explaining why.

SUMMARY OF CHAPTER 15

Children need to be reassured that you love them – and not just with words. You can communicate your love by:

- accepting your child for who he is
- making your child feel special
- being physically affectionate
- using positive body language
- setting limits and boundaries
- giving praise
- being a good listener
- communicating openly.

CHAPTER 16

Family Well-being

However much you care about your partner and love and enjoy your children, family life can have its ups and downs. Mix a variety of personalities and temperaments with life's everyday difficulties and challenges, and there will be good days (laughter, companionship, warmth) and bad (arguments, moods, tension).

Managing work, coping with financial pressures, running a house and at the same time caring for children involves multitasking on a vast range of emotional and practical levels. Finding time to spend together enjoying each other's company can be a challenge, and once you have more than one child, bickering and sniping between siblings can crank up the pressure.

But while expecting bad days is realistic, this doesn't mean that family relationships can't be improved. Often the mood of the house, for example, is set by the parents. If you and your partner are grumpy or constantly quarrelling, chances are your children will pick up on the atmosphere and their own behaviour will deteriorate accordingly. In a household where the parents are kind and respectful towards each other and can deal productively with disagreements, children are more likely to interact with their friends and siblings in the same way, and to be generally more happy and secure.

When it comes to creating family harmony, it makes sense to put your relationship with your partner high on the list of priorities. If your relationship is sound, other challenges, such as dealing with sibling rivalry and finding time for family fun, become so much easier to manage.

Making your relationship work

If you and your partner are happy together – relaxed, affectionate and respectful – chances are your children will be happy (and affectionate and respectful) too.

Creating a stable and happy relationship isn't, however, always easy. From the moment your first baby is born, the dynamics of your relationship will be challenged. You are of two minds – do you put your children first, or your partner first? You may discover qualities in each other you never knew existed (tenderness, patience, one-upmanship, selfishness). Your ideal may have been to work together as a team, while in reality one person may end up doing the lion's share.

Keeping your relationship not just intact but buoyant throughout these years involves real commitment, flexibility and understanding. The key to making it work, for both of you and your children, is discovering how to be both generous (caring for your partner's needs and desires) and assertive (making your own needs and desires known).

● Aim to dole out as many doses of generosity as you can. This not only shows how much you love your partner but also helps you to feel good about yourself.

● Give yourself lots of praise. There will be many times when you have to be your own cheerleader, and you won't always be able to rely on your partner for the feedback you need or deserve. Don't let this come between you. Give yourself a pat on the back instead.

● Avoid trying to 'win'. Relationships have to be partnerships, even if circumstances sometimes mean that they are unequal ones, and competitiveness (always wanting to have the last say, for example) can only ever be destructive.

● Be assertive. If you have a problem, talk about it, and be specific. Say 'I was cross when...' rather than 'You always...'. Don't imagine just because you look grumpy or act prickly that your partner will know what's up.

● Make an effort. With the demands of children and work, the times you have together may be few and far between. It's easy to get lazy. Think about the energy you put into being fun when you're with your friends, and try to do the same with your partner.

● Speak to each other as you wish to be spoken to. Squabbling and bickering can become a habit, creating a depressing atmosphere and a way of interacting which will be copied by your children.

● Keep communicating, not just about the day-to-day stuff, but about your hopes and dreams, likes and dislikes. Conversations in which you share this sort of information will help you to feel close, supported and cared for.

● Don't let practical issues come between you. If household tasks are a cause of conflict, agree to bring in outside help.

● Be realistic. Don't feel guilty about the occasional argument – they are, after all, a fact of life. Seeing you resolve them amicably and constructively will help your children learn how to sort out their own difficulties with you, friends and siblings.

Having fun as a family

Friends and relatives will tell you time and again: 'They grow up so quickly; enjoy them while you can.' And of course, it is true. Childhood, compared to our total life span, is incredibly short. In those early days of broken nights and non-stop nappy changes you may feel time drags, but as your children get older – particularly once they are teenagers – each year will seem to pass in a flash. So, whatever their age, grab all the opportunities you have to have fun and build up a bank of happy memories.

Weekends

Whether or not you work during the week, there are inevitably chores that need doing at the weekend, and children may need taking to and from their own activities. Weekends are supposed to be a chance for relaxing and being together but busy families can sometimes feel as if they are simply spinning in orbit around the house, rarely crossing paths.

Younger children will naturally demand your attention, and will love it if you allocate part of the day over the weekend to a family activity like going for a swim, a cycle ride, a walk or a day out to a nearby attraction. Even simple, more low-key events can make weekends something worth looking forward to. Weekends are a great opportunity for sitting down and eating together, whether it's a big cooked breakfast on Saturday morning or a traditional roast lunch on Sunday.

Other regular treats might include watching a family film together, or going shopping together and stopping at your favourite café for a drink and snack. Routines like these can quickly become part of the fabric of family life and last forever in your child's memory as happy family occasions.

Holidays

Children love holidays, and for obvious reasons. You are away from home and work, and all the responsibilities that go with running a house and holding down a job. And this gives you plenty of free time to spend together as a family. Holidays are also about creating opportunities to do new things in new places and should be fun for everyone. Sometimes, however, spending a condensed amount of time together, especially if your holiday isn't what you expected, can cause friction. So how can you make it work?

- Get in the right frame of mind. If you decide beforehand to have a good time, even if things go wrong (you get lost, children get grumpy, it rains non-stop) you are more likely to be able to laugh and keep the atmosphere happy.

- Don't expect gratitude. Just because you are on holiday and you have gone to so much trouble and expense, your children won't suddenly turn into little angels and be on their best behaviour. There will still be all the normal squabbles – they'll just be about different things.

- Give choices. Holidays should be about everyone having fun, so agree in advance that everybody can choose one thing they'd really love to do and allocate a day or an afternoon to that person's choice.

- And relax. If you are used to rushing about and getting things done, you may find chilling out difficult. Try to remember that being on holiday isn't just about ticking off a list of activities done or sights seen but about having the time to enjoy each other's company.

Managing sibling rivalry

If you have two or more children, sibling rivalry will be a fact of family life. It can range from trivial bickering ('Mum, Martha's squashing me ... eating with her mouth open ... taking ages in the loo') to name calling ('Idiot', 'You're ugly and fat', 'You're both those things and stupid with it!') and aggression (snatching, hitting, poking, prodding).

Why do children fight? Often because it's fun. Often because they believe something is unfair, or they're protecting their territory or their possessions. Sometimes because they are feeling neglected and it gets them attention.

Minor sibling squabbles can be extremely tiresome but on the whole are unlikely to do any lasting damage. More serious or extreme rivalry, however, may be the sign of emotional instability, and could have a big impact on how your child sees herself, and how she relates to others in adult life. For your own sanity, and to help your children form strong and lasting friendships with each other, it makes sense to try to keep upsets to a minimum and to prevent differences getting out of control.

Reducing rivalry

- Aim to love each child uniquely rather than equally. Giving children the individual love, care and attention that suits their own needs will make them feel special rather than just one of a bunch, and help avoid competitiveness.

- Resist labelling. Pigeon-holing your child as 'the clever one', 'the sporty one', 'the cooperative one' or 'the argumentative one' can simply fuel bad feeling between brothers and sisters and become self-fulfilling, denying the individual the motivation to grow and develop new attributes and strengths.

Instead, treat each child as a unique individual with options and opportunities to become whatever she wishes.

- Avoid comparisons. Even if you are doing it with the best of intentions, for example to boost your child's sense of achievement ('You did so much better than your brother'), your child will still feel judged in relation to her sibling and any sense of rivalry will simply be strengthened.

Dealing with fights and arguments

- Outlaw physical aggression of any sort. Adopting a policy of zero tolerance when it comes to snatching, hitting, scratching and punching from the earliest age helps put the message across loud and clear.

- If fighting does occur, remind children of the house rules and separate them. Tell them both to go their rooms until they have calmed down.

- Look for a pattern. If fights or arguments always happen at the same time of day or over the same issue, find ways to change the routine or sort out the issue.

- When there are arguments, try not to interfere. Unless it looks like it's going to escalate into something physical, it's better to give your children the chance to learn how to settle disputes peacefully.

- Avoid becoming piggy in the middle. Asking questions like 'Who started it?' or 'Why has this happened?' will simply rope you into the argument, fuel the anger and prolong the fight.

- If you need to step in, start by simply describing the problem ('Okay, there's only one biscuit left and you both want it') without taking sides or judging. Then tell your children that you are confident they can sort it out, and leave them to it.

SUMMARY OF CHAPTER 16

Family life is bound to have both highs and lows. Pressures from inside and outside the home can mean that family harmony is hard to find, but it is the responsibility of parents. The following can help:

- Make your relationship with your partner work.
- Take all the opportunities you find to have fun as a family.
- Make the most of weekends and holidays to spend time as a family.
- Deal with sibling rivalry by making individual children feel special and by avoiding more serious rivalry and any form of physical aggression.

CHAPTER 17

Into the Wider World

At 18 your child is, officially, an adult. Legally he is no longer your responsibility. But of course, in reality, he's still young and inexperienced. Whatever he chooses to do with his life, go away to college or start a job, he's going to face difficult decisions and make mistakes. He needs to know that you are always on hand to offer emotional support and, for a while at least, probably financial support too.

Helping your adult child at this stage in your life won't always be easy. This is partly because it can be so hard to let go. You've done a great job and helped your child grow into an independent and capable adult, but it's difficult to shake off the feeling that he depends on you for his happiness and well-being and that without your constant advice and guidance, he will make a mess of things. Maybe this will happen, but your adult child won't thank you for interfering. Instead you need to wait to be asked for your advice, and be generous with your help if things go wrong.

Accepting your child as an adult, free to make his own choices and decisions, can be hard, especially if you've been a full-time stay-at-home mum, your life revolving around your child's schedule – running him over to his friends, helping him with his coursework, waiting up for him after a night out. Once he leaves home, even if it's just to go away to college, the house can seem deafeningly quiet.

Adjusting to life once your child has left home can, for some mothers, be hard. You may wonder what role you have to play now that he no longer needs you day to day. But recognising that you are and always will be his mother, and he will always want and need your love and support, whatever his age, will be hugely sustaining. Life can still be good, and your relationship with your adult child can still be good.

The irony, of course, is that having made the adjustment to life at home without your child, research shows that there's a good chance he'll soon be back. Nowadays, mainly for financial reasons such as student debts and the difficulty of getting on the housing ladder, around one in five British adults still lives in the family home.

Supporting your adult child

Your grown-up child has many important decisions and new experiences ahead of him. He may be off to university, planning a gap year or starting his first job. Whatever he chooses to do, he'll need to fend for himself – manage his own chores, handle his own money and establish his own relationships. But this doesn't mean you have no part to play. As long as your child feels he can come to you for help and support without being judged, your relationship will be as strong as ever.

- Encourage him to think about leaving home. Whether it is to go off to university, take a gap year and travel the world, or start a new job and share a flat with friends, now is the time for your grown-up child to spread his wings and find his independence.

- Make sure he knows how to fend for himself, especially when it comes to cooking. Knowing how to make simple, inexpensive but nutritious meals will help him to stay healthy and make friends!

- Be available when he needs you. Even the most confident young adult can find leaving home and starting a new life daunting. If you're too busy to talk on the phone or can't be contacted, he could feel insecure and unsettled.

- Only offer advice when asked. At this age, your child needs to make his own decisions, and his own mistakes. Always giving unwanted advice will be seen as interference and will be resented.

- When you are asked for advice don't expect it to be taken. Your child may simply be looking for another point of view that helps to put his own ideas and thoughts into perspective.

- If you enjoy being involved in your child's life, offer practical help. Give him a lift back to college at the beginning and end of term, help him to decorate his new room, bake him a cake to take back to his digs.

- Be positive about his life choices even if you personally would do something different. Remember that just because he's your child, he's under no obligation to share your values or beliefs.

Coping with empty nest syndrome

There are some mums who rub their hands in glee at the freedom they gain when their grown-up child leaves home for the first time, and there are other mums who feel a great sense of loss and sadness. When the latter happens, 'empty nest syndrome' as it is often called may last for days or even weeks.

It can be hard to bear, but for your own and your child's sake you need to accept that although life has changed, it's not over. You are still a mum, but now you need to take a back-seat role. And just as your child needs to find his way in his new life and forge his independence, so do you. Deal first with the practicalities of your child's departure and then work on being as positive as you can.

- Plan ahead. The initial silence in the house, especially when your youngest leaves home, can be deafening, so organise distractions. Invite visitors to come and stay, take a short break with your partner or friends, get yourself signed up on an evening or day-time course that starts at the same time as the university term.

- Don't make leaving home difficult for your child by being clingy or showing that you are upset. This is a significant step in your child's life and he needs your encouragement and support.

- Stay in contact but don't swamp your child with phone calls. Agree a time once or twice a week when you will make contact with each other (you could help by buying some credit for his mobile phone).

- If you find it hard not to get emotional on the phone, send a text or an email instead.

- Don't jump at the chance of suggesting your child gives up and comes home if he's finding it hard to settle or sounds miserable. It's inevitable that it will take time for him to get used to life away from home, and he needs you to remind him of this.

- Cope with the initial separation by doing all the things you haven't had a chance to do for so long – long lie-ins, watching your favourite television show, eating the food you love, redecorating (but leave your child's bedroom, as he'll need to feel he has a base for sometime yet).

- Remind yourself that just because life is different doesn't mean it can't be as good, then make some positive long-term plans. Organise an amazing trip, get involved in a cause you feel passionate about, learn a new skill, start a new hobby or plot some excitement and challenges into the following year. This will keep you from moping around the house and encourage you to see your life through fresh eyes.

> *'When we came back after settling James into his room for his first term at university I was distraught. I kept bursting into tears, and would find myself just standing in his bedroom to feel closer to him.'*
>
> Anne, mum to James, aged 19

Keeping the door ajar

For your grown-up child's healthy development, you need to make it as easy as possible for him to fly the nest. But while he's finding his feet out in the big wide world, it's equally important for him to know that he can return home if he needs to.

Of course, some children find it easy to barge back into their parents' lives with a load of washing and a request for a slap-up meal. Others may find it harder, possibly feeling ashamed or embarrassed to ask for help (if they've failed an exam, chosen the wrong course, lost their job); or thinking that you are too busy and have your own commitments or problems to deal with.

Offering a safe, if temporary, haven to your child when he needs an extra dose of love and security is, for most parents, acceptable. But nowadays, financial pressures too can force many young people to return home. Rising house prices in particular have resulted in around one in four young people between the ages of 20 and 30 still living with their parents. When this happens, being supportive and caring – while ensuring your goodwill isn't being abused – can involve a fine balancing act.

- When your child leaves home, make sure he always knows where you are and can get in contact with you if necessary. If he thinks you are fussing over him, tell him it's for your peace of mind.

- Remind him that his needs are still your main concern. Even grown-up children need to be reassured that they are loved, and loved unconditionally.

- Tell him that he shouldn't feel embarrassed or worried about coming back if circumstances make this necessary, but be positive too, and let him know that if this does happen you are sure any setbacks will only be temporary.

- Make it plain that if he does need to return home, you know he won't take advantage of you. Reassure him, for example, that there will always be a bed for him at home, and that you know he will pay his way if he can.

- If your child does have to come back home, it's important for both of you to maintain a respectful relationship and avoid resentment building up. Tell him that you know it must be hard for him living back at home again, and then suggest that together you look at ways of making it easier for everyone. Then gently raise issues such as how long he thinks he'll be staying, how he can contribute financially, whether he can take on some chores, etc. Even if you are delighted to have him back, remind yourself that he still needs to be working towards independence.

SUMMARY OF CHAPTER 17

Your child is, officially, an adult, but he'll still need your emotional support for a while yet.

- Encourage him to spread his wings and leave home, but prepare him for this and make sure he knows you are there if you are needed.

- Cope with 'empty nest syndrome' by reminding yourself that you are still a mum, but now you have time for yourself, and your own future.

- Keep the door ajar. If he has difficulties, he needs to know he can always come home again, but if this does happen, be sure to talk about how it will work – emotionally and practically – for you both.

CHAPTER 18

When Things Go Wrong

Sometimes our lives don't turn out as we expect them to. However much you have longed to have a family you may have to face many struggles along the way. Many early pregnancies, for example, end in miscarriage. And even more marriages end in divorce. But with the right help and support it may still be possible to achieve your dreams and have a fulfilling family life.

Miscarriage

This is one of the most common pregnancy complications. Around one in five pregnancies end in miscarriage, with most occurring during the first 12 weeks. Around this time, when your period is due, it's not unusual to experience some spotting. But heavier bleeding and cramp-like pains could be a sign of miscarriage.

- Always contact your midwife or doctor if you experience bleeding. You may be told to rest and 'wait and see'. Alternatively you may be sent to hospital for an ultrasound scan. If you are told that your cervix has begun to dilate it's unlikely that your pregnancy will be able to continue.

- Miscarrying in very early pregnancy often requires no treatment, although sometimes a minor operation (a D&C, or dilatation and curettage) may be necessary to empty the uterus.

- Allow yourself time to recover, both physically and emotionally. Although you may feel that getting pregnant again is the best solution, you will probably be advised to wait until you have had two or three periods.

- Don't let others brush aside your feelings. Miscarriage can be a trauma, even when it occurs early in the pregnancy.

- Try not to be angry. You may feel that your body has let you down but most miscarriages occur for no identifiable reason, which is why investigations into the possible causes of miscarriage are usually only offered to women who have had three or more miscarriages.

- Talk about how you feel with someone who knows what you are going through. Realising that you are not alone, and that there are many other women who have experienced miscarriage too, can be extremely comforting.

- If you are finding it hard to get over a miscarriage, or just need extra support or advice, contact the Miscarriage Association (see Further Sources of Information, page 153).

'I lost my first pregnancy at ten weeks, and I was terrified I might never have a baby. But I was told my chances of a successful pregnancy were just as high as before the miscarriage. Now I'm pregnant again – 18 weeks – and so far so good.'

Jennifer, aged 27

Stillbirth and neonatal death

For a baby to die before the end of pregnancy, or shortly after birth, is devastating. Progressively throughout your pregnancy the bond you develop with your baby becomes stronger and stronger. To lose that baby just as you expect to be carrying her home is cruel beyond belief, even if you know in advance that your baby has died, or won't survive the birth.

Stillbirth is rare. Only about five babies in 1000 are stillborn. The main causes are infection, placental problems, problems with the mother's health, congenital malformations and complications surrounding the umbilical cord.

How you deal with stillbirth will be a very personal matter.

- You will be offered the opportunity to hold your baby to say goodbye and to take photographs and even a lock of hair if you wish. Some parents find the prospect of doing this unbearable, but for others if can be hugely comforting. Try to think ahead as you don't want to have regrets later.

- Get a friend or family member to tell everyone who needs to know what has happened. It's too much to expect you or your partner to have to go through the details again and again.

- Before you leave the hospital make sure your doctor gives you tablets for stopping your milk coming in. Even if you lose your baby early in your pregnancy, this is likely to happen and will only add to the trauma.

- Expect to grieve for a long time. You will feel deeply shocked by what you've experienced, as well as bereft. You may need support for many months.

- Prepare yourself for when you go out in case you meet someone who knew you were pregnant but who doesn't know the outcome. Tell them you 'had a baby girl, but she didn't live'.

- If people avoid you, try not to take it personally. For those who have never experienced loss, knowing what to say or do can be difficult. There is often the worry that mentioning it will bring back the sorrow, although most parents who experience stillbirth agree that they would rather their loss were acknowledged than ignored.

> *'My first baby was born, and died, at 28 weeks. I was numb with the shock and horror of what was happening, but I forced myself to hold her, and we took a photo. Now, ten years later, I have three wonderful children, but I've still not been able to look at that photo.'*
>
> Tessa, mum to Emily, aged nine, Rory, aged seven, and Oliver, aged four

- Remember that your partner will be suffering too, although he may express his sorrow in a different way. Try to keep talking, and support each other.

- Don't be afraid to accept help. You may be offered counselling by your health service; alternatively you may prefer to turn to your church, your family or your friends.

- For support from parents who have also experienced stillbirth or neonatal death, contact SANDS, the Stillbirth and Neonatal Death Society (see Further Sources of Information, page 153).

Separation and divorce

Today, around one in four children experiences the break-up of their family. When this happens, children's lives are, inevitably, turned upside down. And while very young children may often readily accept new domestic arrangements, as they grow and develop there will continually be issues that need to be handled carefully and sensitively in order to minimise the harm and suffering.

Children can experience a whole range of emotions when their parents break up, from guilt and anger, to rejection and loss of self-esteem. Initially their behaviour may deteriorate, they may be less cooperative and find it hard to concentrate at school. Some children, particularly boys, may find it hard to express their feelings.

Children who experience conflict between their parents may feel their loyalties are being pulled in two directions. Seeing a parent distressed is tremendously upsetting and unsettling. And teenagers can take separation especially hard. At a time when they are struggling to find their own identity, losing the stability of family life may only add to their sense of confusion.

Once separation is inevitable, it's more often than not the father who leaves the family home. It's vital, however, for the sake of your child's happiness that she continues her relationship with him. Research highlights the huge impact a father's involvement in his child's life can have both on the child's emotional well-being and progress at school. If you find it hard to discuss these kinds of issues with your partner, outside mediation may help to avoid legal action, which is expensive, can drag on, and ultimately may not even sort matters out.

No one would wish for their child to have to experience the pain and disruption caused by separation and divorce, but by handling the situation carefully and sensitively it is possible to minimise the damage.

- Make a plan with your partner. Decide how you can continue to parent your children together, taking into account the need for flexibility (as children grow, their needs change). Discuss too keeping up contact with the wider family as children shouldn't have to lose contact with grandparents, aunts, uncles and cousins.

- Talk to your children throughout the process. Explain what's happening, why it's happening (without blaming either parent) and stress that it's not their fault. Separation can affect children's confidence, so continual reassurance is important.

- Encourage your children to discuss their feelings too – but don't force them – and accept their feelings (see Being a good listener, page 131).

'My ex-partner can make life very difficult but for the sake of my boys I avoid getting drawn into a fight. Sometimes this means swallowing my pride but it's worth it.'

Lauren, mum to Josh, aged five, and Simon, aged nine

- Reassure your children that you can cope. Children only feel safe and secure when they sense that their parents are in control, and they don't need to worry.

- Find other families who have been through separation too: knowing there are other children in a similar situation will help them to accept the situation.

- Don't poison your children against your ex. They need to be free to love him, without feeling that they'll be letting you down.

● If you start a new relationship, you may well face hostility from your children. This is normal. They need time to adjust so take it gradually. Once they can see that you are happy and that their relationship with you isn't being affected, they will come to accept the idea.

SUMMARY OF CHAPTER 18

- Miscarriage, even in the early stages of pregnancy, can be traumatic. Give yourself time to recover.
- Stillbirth and neonatal death are devastating. You will be deeply shocked and bereft and will grieve for a long time. Get plenty of emotional support.
- Separation and divorce are difficult for children but the impact can be reduced by working with your partner, ensuring that your children still have contact with both parents and by talking to and reassuring your children throughout the process.

Further Sources of Information

Pregnancy and birth

The Active Birth Centre
25 Bickerton Road
London N19 5JT
Tel: 020 7281 6760
www.activebirthcentre.com
Information and classes on natural
active childbirth

ARC (Antenatal Results and Choices)
84–88 Pinner Road
Harrow
Middlesex HA1 4HZ
Tel: 020 7631 0285
www.arc-uk.org
Information and support around
antenatal testing and when an
abnormality is diagnosed

BLISS (Baby Life Support Systems)
1st Floor
68 South Lambeth Road
London SW8 1RL
Tel: 0500 618140 (9.30am–5pm
weekdays)
General enquiries: 0870 7700337
www.bliss.org.uk
Helpline for parents of premature
and special needs babies

The Maternity Alliance
45 Beech Street
London EC2P 2LX
Tel: 020 7588 8582
www.maternityalliance.org.uk
Advice and information about
maternity rights and benefits

Anna McGrail and Daphne Metland,
*Expecting – Everything you need to
know about pregnancy, labour and
birth*, Virago Press, 1-94408-034-X

Miscarriage Association
c/o Clayton Hospital
Northgate
Wakefield
West Yorkshire WF1 3JS
Tel: 01924 200799
www.miscarriageassocation.org.uk
Advice and information on a
national network of miscarriage
support groups

National Childbirth Trust
Alexandra House
Oldham Terrace
Acton
London W3 6NH
Tel: 0870 4448707
www.nctpregnancyandbaby
care.cpm
Antenatal classes and postnatal help

NHS Smoking in Pregnancy Helpline
Tel: 0800 1690 169
Support to help stop smoking

SANDS (Stillbirth and Neonatal Death
Society)
28 Portland Place
London W1B 1LY
Tel: 020 7436 5881
www.uk-sands.org
National support network for
bereaved parents

Vegetarian Society
Parkdale
Durham Road
Altrincham
Cheshire WA14 4QG
Tel: 0161 928 0793
www.vegsoc.org
For information on vegetarian diets
during pregnancy and for infants

Baby and childcare

Association of Breastfeeding Mothers
PO Box 207
Bridgwater TA6 7YT
Tel: 020 7813 1481
www.home.clara.net/abm
Information, encouragement and
support for breastfeeding mothers,
mothers-to-be and their families

Association for Post Natal Illness
145 Dawes Road
London SW6 7EB
Tel: 020 7386 0868
www.apni.org
Advice for women with post-natal
depression

BLISS (Baby Life Support Systems)
1st Floor
68 South Lambeth Road
London SW8 1RL
Tel: 0500 618140 (9.30am–5pm
weekdays)
General enquiries: 0870 7700337
www.bliss.org.uk
Helpline for parents of premature
and special needs babies

Dr Jane Collins (consultant editor),
Baby and Child Health, Dorling
Kindersley,
1-4053-0063-9

Dr Carol Cooper (consultant editor),
Johnson's Mother and Baby, Dorling
Kindersley,
9-78-140531469-5

CRY-SIS
BM CRY-SIS
London WC1N 3XX
Tel: 020 7404 5011
Advice on babies who cry
excessively

Dorothy Einon, *Child Behaviour*,
Viking, 0-670-85968-0

Family Rights Group
The Print House
18 Ashwin Street
London E8 3DL
Tel: 0800 731 1696 (free and
confidential advice, 10–12pm and
1.30–3.30pm weekdays)
Email: advice@frg.org.uk
www.frg.org.uk
Advice and support for families
whose children are involved with
social services

Family Welfare Association
501-505 Kingsland Road
London E8 4AU
Tel: 020 7254 6251
Email: fwa.headoffice@fwa.org.uk
www.fwa.org.uk
Support for poorer families,
providing grants and social work
advice

For Parents by Parents
c/o 31 Main Street
Bishopstone
Aylesbury
Buckinghamshire HP17 8SF
Tel: 01296 747551
Email: contributions@forparents
byparents.com
www.forparentsbyparents.com
A UK parenting site, funded and
maintained by parents

Gingerbread
7 Sovereign Court
Sovereign Place
London E1W 3HW
Tel: 0800 018 4318 (10am–3pm
weekdays)
www.gingerbread.org.uk
Advice and support for one-parent
families

Home-Start
2 Salisbury Road
Leicester LE1 7QR
Tel: 0116 2339955
www.home-start.org.uk

Provides emotional and practical support to families with at least one child under the age of five years in their own home

La Leche League
BM 3424
London WC1N 3XX
Tel: 020 7242 1278
www.laleche.org.uk
Helpline for breastfeeding advice and information, open weekdays 9am–8pm

Gael Lindenfield, *Confident Teens*, Thorsons, 0-00-710062-0

MAMA (Meet-a-mum Association)
376 Bideford Green
Linsdael
Leighton Buzzard
Bedfordshire LU72TY
Tel: 01761 433598
Helpline: 020 8768 0123 (7–10pm weekdays)
www.mama.org.uk
Advice and support for isolated and depressed mothers

Mothers Over 40
www.mothersover40.com
Online advice and support for older mums and dads

National Childbirth Trust
Alexandra House
Oldham Terrace
Acton
London W3 6NH
Tel: 0870 4448707
www.nctpregnancyandbaby care.com
Antenatal classes and postnatal help

National Childminding Association
8 Masons Hill
Bromley
Kent BR2 9EY
Tel: 020 8464 6164
www.ncma.org.uk

National Council for One Parent Families
255 Kentish Town Road
London NW5 2LX
Tel: 0800 018 5026
www.oneparentfamilies.org.uk
Information and advice for lone parents

NSPCC
Weston House
42 Curtain Road
London EC2A 3NH
Helpline: 0808 800 5000
Email: help@nspcc.org.uk
www.nspcc.org.uk
Parent and family support

Parentline Plus
250 Highgate Studios
53-79 Highgate Road
London NW5ITL
Tel: 0808 800 2222
www.parentlineplus.org.uk
Support and information for parents

Jan Parker and Jan Simpson, *Sibling Rivalry, Sibling Love*, Hodder Mobius, 0-340-79346-5

Raising Kids
www.raisingkids.co.uk

Single Parents
www.singleparents.org.uk
Online community with information, advice, first-hand experiences and details of local groups

TAMBA (Twins and Multiple Birth Association)
2 The Willows
Gardner Road
Guildford
Surrey GU1 4PG
Tel: 0870 770 3305
Helpline: 01732 868000
www.tamba.org.uk
Support and information for families of twins, triplets and more

Vegetarian Society
Parkdale
Durham Road
Altrincham
Cheshire WA14 4QG
Tel: 0161 928 0793
www.vegsoc.org
For information on vegetarian diets during pregnancy and for infants

Child health and nutrition

Allergy UK
Deepdene House
30 Bellegrove Road
Welling
Kent DA16 3PY
Tel: 020 8303 8525
www.allergyuk.org

Catherine Atkinson, *Start Right Baby and Toddler Meal Planning*, Foulsham, 0-572-02974-8

Joanna Blythman, *The Food Our Children Eat*, Fourth Estate, 1-857-02936-4

British Dietetic Association
Charles House
5th Floor
148–149 Great Charles Street
Queensway
Birmingham B3 3HT
Tel: 0121 200 8080
www.bda.uk.com

British Nutrition Foundation
High Holborn House
52–54 High Holborn
London WC1V 6RQ
Tel: 020 7404 6504
www.nutrition.org.uk

Child Accident Prevention Trust
18–20 Farringdon Lane
London EC1R 3HA
Tel: 020 7608 3828
www.capt.org.uk

NHS Direct
Tel: 0845 4647 (24 hours a day, seven days a week)
For immediate advice on any concerns you may have about yourself or your baby

Ellen Shanley and Colleen Thompson, *Fuelling the Teen Machine*, Bull Publishing, 0-923-52157-7

Peter Vaughan, *Simply Better Food for your Baby and Children*, Foulsham, 0-572-03003-7

Relationships

Alan Bradley and Jody Beveridge, *How to Help the Children Survive the Divorce*, Foulsham, 0-572-02956-X

Relate
Herbert Grey College
Little Church Street
Rugby
Warwickshire CV21 3AP
Tel: 01788 573241
www.relate.org.uk
Provides information on local Relate centres, offering counselling help for marriage and family relationship needs

OnDivorce
Tel: 0906 9060250 (Speak to a specialist lawyer, £1.50 per minute, 8–10pm
seven days a week)
www.ondivorce.co.uk
Resource for those experiencing divorce

Work

Maternity Alliance
Third floor West
2–6 Northburgh Street
London EC1V 0AY
Tel: 020 7490 7638
www.maternityalliance.org.uk

Parents at work
45 Beech Street
London EC2Y 8AD
Tel: 020 7628 3565
www.parentsatwork.org.uk
Helping working parents and their employers find a better balance between responsibilities at home and at work

Steve Wharton, *High-vibrational Thinking: How to Get Back to Work*, Foulsham, 0-572-03078-9

Steve Wharton, *High-vibrational Thinking: How to Restore Your Life–work Balance*, Foulsham, 0-572-03077-0

Working Families
1–3 Berry Street
London EC1V 0AA
Tel: 020 7253 7243
Email: office@working families.org.uk
www.workingfamilies.org.uk
Information for working families and employers

For children and teenagers

Brook Advisory Centre
Tel: 0800 018 5023
www.brook.org.uk

Childline
Tel: 0800 1111 (24-hour free helpline)
www.childline.org.uk
Confidential advice

Eating Disorders Association
103 Prince of Wales Road
Norwich NR1 1DW
Youthline: 0845 634 7650 (callers aged 18 and under, 4–6.30pm weekdays, 1–4.30pm Saturday)
Email: talkback@edauk.com
Adult helpline: 0845 634 1414 (8.30am–8.30pm weekdays, 1–4.30pm Saturday)

Email: helpmail@edauk.com
www.edauk.com
Information and support regarding eating disorders

Frank
Tel: 0800 77 66 00 (free and confidential, 24 hours a day, seven days a week)
Textphone: FRANK 0800 917 8765
Email: frank@talktofrank.com
www.talktofrank.com
Confidential drug information and advice

Robie H Harris, *Let's Talk About Sex*, Walker Books, 1-844-28174-4 (illustrated guide to growing up for children aged 8–14)

Kidscape
2 Grosvenor Gardens
London SW1W ODH
Tel: 020 7730 330
www.kidscape.org.uk
Charity to prevent child abuse and bullying

National Self-Harm Network
www.nshn.co.uk

Sexwise
Tel: 0800 28 29 30
www.ruthinking.co.uk
Free, confidential advice

Steve Wharton, *High-vibrational Thinking: How to Stop that Bully*, Foulsham, 0-572-03075-4

Young Minds
102–108 Clerkenwell Road
London EC1H 5SA
Tel: 0800 018 2138 (Young Minds Parents' information service)
www.youngminds.org.uk
Mental health support for the young

Index